MOTHER'S INGREDIENTS

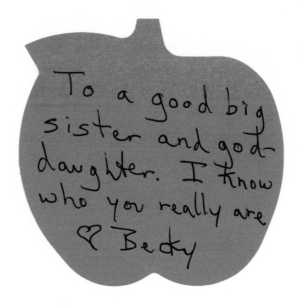

To a good big sister and god-daughter. I know who you really are ♥ Becky

Mother's Ingredients

A memoir
by

TARA CUMMINS

Adelaide Books
New York / Lisbon
2020

MOTHER'S INGREDIENTS
A memoir
By Tara Cummins

Copyright © by Tara Cummins
Cover design © 2020 Adelaide Books

Published by Adelaide Books, New York / Lisbon
adelaidebooks.org
Editor-in-Chief
Stevan V. Nikolic

For any information, please address Adelaide Books
at info@adelaidebooks.org
or write to:
Adelaide Books
244 Fifth Ave. Suite D27
New York, NY, 10001

ISBN: 978-1-951896-60-7
Printed in the United States of America

Although this work contains descriptions of people in my life, many of their names and other identifying characteristics have been changed to protect their privacy.

For my family: Iche liebe dich.

And for the little ones I created: I love you more than words.

Contents

Prologue

The quiet waiting room with its white walls and light blue tiles makes me squirm in my seat. I try to distract myself by watching the other women in the office, but their big bellies and pregnancy magazines make me even more anxious.

A nurse opens the door and calls out a name, but I don't hear it. I think about how I'm pregnant and how excited and utterly terrifying that is. I stare at my stomach and wonder if it should feel different. Shouldn't I somehow instinctually feel that I'm pregnant? Should mother's intuition have kicked in yet? My stomach doesn't look any different and it doesn't feel any different, but there is a tiny life blooming within.

A sharp nudge from Alex, my husband, pulls me from my thoughts.

"She's calling you, babe. You ready?" His bright blue eyes look happy. They literally shine. He is the most attractive man I have ever seen, and he is how I got here waiting to see a doctor.

"Sure," I say sounding timid. I stand up and suddenly feel ashamed that I'm so nervous. It's not that I don't want to be a mother, it's just that the thought of becoming a mother chills me deep down to my core. I think about my mother. Dark rooms and sweaty faces fill my mind and I desperately try to shove those memories away as I smile at the nurse.

"We will be in the second exam room. I left a robe in there for you, so just change into it and I will be back in a moment." She points to the room and walks back to the nurse's station.

I take a deep breath and change quickly into the robe. There is a large machine next to the bed and I try not to bump it while I climb up. I spin my wedding ring around my finger nervously, a habit I picked up right after getting married a year and a half ago. Closing my eyes, I imagine what my baby will look like. I hope it has Alex's thick hair and sunny smile. I can almost see a small child with bright blue eyes with yellow around the iris and big feet for playing soccer. Hopefully it will be smart and have a sense of humor, and maybe even like to read like me.

I don't know a single thing about being a mother, or caring for a child around the clock, but somehow my fears are replaced with a desperate longing to hold my baby. Maybe when I become a mom, I can undo some of the damage my mother did to me. Maybe I can be better for my child and break the chain of abuse that seems to follow my mother and her family. I say a silent prayer and finish just as the door opens.

"Mrs. Cummins, my name is Jessica and I'll be the technician today. Have you ever had an ultrasound before?" She sits on a stool next to the large machine and flips on a button. The monitor turns a fuzzy grey and it shakes a little. Her wrinkled fingers fly over dozens of unmarked knobs and buttons before she looks up at me. She has obviously been doing this a long time.

"No. First time." I say. She smiles, and her face reminds me of a broken mirror with deep wrinkles and cracks spreading from her mouth.

"Alright, well lay down and pull your gown up. I will cover your privates with a sheet and then we can get started."

I scoot back onto the bed and lay down. She hands me a sheet and I clumsily pull my gown up. The air is cold, and I feel awkward, but she helps me cover up quickly and sits back onto her stool.

"Now just verify your date of birth for me."

"February 12, 1991."

"Oh wow, you're only 21. I expected you to be older since you're already married." She says pulling on some gloves.

I don't really know what to say so I just smile and nod.

"I got married pretty young too. We met in college and then we got pregnant and I dropped out to raise the baby. Then we got pregnant again and I pushed off going to school. We decided to have me work and help support him while he went to medical school and then I got pregnant again, but this time with a boy, and when he was a few years old his dad graduated medical school, got a great internship, met a beautiful little nurse and left me," she laughs. "This is just some lubrication jelly. I tried to put it in the warmer, but that thing hasn't been working right so it might still be cold. I'm going to put it on your abdomen before we start the ultrasound."

She holds out the tube and shows me. I like how much she talks, despite her choice of story. It takes the pressure from me and I find it soothing to know exactly what she is going to be doing before she does it.

"Here we go." She squeezes it and bright blue jelly falls onto my stomach. It's warm and she spreads it around for a second with her hand.

"Alright, now I'm going to use this wand and press it onto your stomach. It might feel a little weird, but it shouldn't hurt. There could be times where I have to press harder, so if you feel like you have to pee just let me know."

I nod and watch as she presses the half-moon shaped piece onto my stomach. Will I be able to discern a baby through all the rest of the tissue? I turn my head and watch the monitor. All I see are lumps of dark grey next to lumps of a lighter grey color. I can't tell what anything is, so I just close my eyes and wait for the technician to let me know how things are going.

"I'm going to let you hear the heartbeat first and then I will measure the baby and show you where everything is." She presses down near my belly button and a soft rhythmic pulse fills the room. It sounds like nothing I have ever heard before and I'm amazed. Amazed that there is a tiny heart pumping blood around a tiny baby. In that instant I feel connected to that small life inside of me. The tension I have been feeling melts away with each tiny beat of the little heart.

"Hmm, there is a little interference, did you eat recently?" She moves the wand down further and moves it from side to side.

"Yeah, I ate an hour ago."

"It's probably just your digestive track. Now how far along did your doctor say you were?"

"At my last appointment he said that I was around 18 weeks."

"Mmm-hmmm. Now let me start the measurements," She pauses for a second, "Yeah, here is the little arm. Let's measure that." I smile and imagine five miniature fingers and five tiny nails. The technician presses down hard, and it tickles a little. She taps a button a few times, the machine whirls and she takes a sharp breath.

My eyes pop open. I look at her face and see her intently looking at the screen. Her fingers fly over the buttons while she presses the wand onto different areas of my stomach. She is silent.

I wait for her to start chatting again, but minutes go by with only the clicking of the buttons and our breathing to fill the void. There must be something horribly wrong for her to be so quiet. My mind goes into overdrive. Maybe there are just extra fingers on the baby or there could be a hole in the little heart. Hopefully the baby just isn't growing a limb. I could live with a baby who was missing a leg or an arm. That wouldn't be so bad.

I try to calm down by reminding myself that I heard the heartbeat. I know the baby is alive. But anxiety fills me, and I can't stop thinking about what might be wrong. Maybe I'm not going to become a mom after all. I feel like my limbs weigh hundreds of pounds and my chest is heavy with terror.

I spin my wedding ring around trying to stay calm. The technicians face seems to be frozen as she stares at the screen. She presses down on my stomach, hard, and I try not to breath. If I'm still, she may be able to work better.

The silence stretches on and I can't take it after fifteen minutes. "Is everything alright?" I ask.

She pulls the tube of lubricant back out, squeezes a thin line on top of her wand and looks back at me. "Oh yeah. Some of these measurements are just kind of difficult and I have to focus." She smiles for a second before starting work again.

I stare up at the white ceiling and count my breaths. If I focus on the rush of air that fills my lungs and the quiet whoosh of it leaving, I don't have to think about anything else. I don't know how long I lay there, but eventually the clicking of the buttons slow and stop.

"Well, I'm going to go bring your husband in here and then I can show you what's going on. Just hold on another minute," She says, backing out of the door.

I hear Alex's voice down the hall and try to smile at him when he walks in, but I'm too afraid about what is probably wrong with the baby to make it look realistic.

"How's it going?" He asks.

"Fine." I try to let him know something is wrong with my tone, without saying anything in front of the technician.

He automatically raises his eyebrows and reaches for me. As his thumb rubs small circles on the back of my hand, I feel a rush a relief. I never believed in soulmates, or true love, or even happy marriages before I met Alex. Somehow being near him and knowing he will be there for me makes me feel like I can conquer anything. I'm thankful that he was able to help shift my pessimistic view on love.

Our technician pulls on some new gloves and grabs another tube of lubrication. She puts a big pile of it right near my belly button and says, "Well I would ask if you wanted to find out the gender, but you aren't that far along yet."

Alex's eyebrows furrow and I know what he must be thinking. At 18 weeks we should be able to find out the gender. His mother was a labor and delivery nurse for years and then became the head of maternal and fetal research at one of the best hospitals in the area. She told us that we could find out the gender today and to come by her house on the way home to tell everyone.

"But I thought you could see the gender as early as fifteen weeks?" I ask.

"That's true but your uterus is larger than normal, and the doctor was wrong about how far along you are. You're actually only about 10 weeks."

My uterus is bigger than normal? What does that even mean? I look up at Alex and he squeezes my hand.

"What does that mean?" His voice is strained, and I know he's worried.

"Well how about I show you, alright?" She turns the monitor to face us and presses down with her wand. I automatically have the urge to pee, but I hold it in and try not to move too much.

"Alright, well if you look at the screen you will be able to see your baby."

The screen is all grey, but right in the middle is a weird white blob. There's a definite skull with little black holes where the eyes will grow and a tiny spine that is a perfect straight line connected to four perfect limbs. It almost looks like a little alien. As I watch it, the technician presses down a little more and my baby wiggles.

I know that right now it doesn't look like a baby and that it wouldn't survive on its own, but I'm automatically filled with love and an intense desire to protect it. This thing growing inside of me has made me feel extremely sick for weeks and will continue to do so, but I don't care. I can't take my eyes off it. I love it instantly and completely.

"Well the baby is growing perfectly and is right on schedule. The reason your uterus is bigger is right here. Look at the screen," She moves her wand around and then smiles, "and here is another one. Growing perfectly and right in tune with its sibling."

On screen is another little alien baby with four limbs and a big skull. The images become a little fuzzy for a second and then there are two little babies right next to each other. They wiggle in unison and I can't take my eyes off them.

"Twins?" Alex whispers.

"Yep. They are in their own amniotic sac and they have their own placenta which is the best way to have twins. They won't steal nutrients from each other, and it will be safer for them."

Jessica smiles as she shows us the placentas and each baby's measurements. She is bubbly again and chatting away.

I look up at Alex and his eyes are wide. I know he must be freaking out as much as I am. Instead of becoming a mom to one baby, I will have to figure out how to do it with two little ones. I was hoping to breastfeed, but with two babies I don't know if I will be able to. What if my body doesn't produce enough milk? I know that there is always formula, but nursing seems like the best way to go. And if I can't breastfeed how are we ever going to afford to feed two babies? Let alone buy double the clothes, diapers, care seats, and cribs.

And now that there are two babies, we must bring back the single stroller and buy a double one instead. My mind starts to race with all the preparations needed to welcome two infants at once.

Motherhood is such a great responsibly, I don't know if I will be able to be everything my children need me to be. I don't have a good example to follow, and I'm nervous about figuring it all out by myself. I feel overwhelmed.

"Well you're pretty lucky! You'll have three heads and six arms and six legs for nine months! And that is why the doctor thought you were further along in your pregnancy, because there are two in there. You are technically measuring at what a singleton pregnancy would be at 18 weeks." The technician smiles and looks at me.

I smile and think about how strange it will be to grow two babies. Dread fills my stomach. Or maybe I'm just hungry. The thought of food makes me feel nauseous and I have to close my eyes and hold my breath for a minute for it all to go away.

Playing Chase

Mom is facing the other way and scrubbing the kitchen floor with a toothbrush. I'm four years old and live at 461 Pine Drive in Crestline, California. Our small mountain community is nestled into the San Bernardino National Forrest and sits at about 4550 feet elevation. The town is split in half by Lake Gregory and has one family owned grocery store, Goodwin's Market. The town is a strange place where middle class working families mix with the impoverished who often struggle with addictions. The one elementary school is filled with all the children of both groups and a place where, for the most part, everyone gets along despite your background. I have to wait another year until I can go to school there. My older sister Emma is in the third grade and is there every day. Dad goes to college too, so it's just me and Mom during the day.

I watch Mom climb onto the counter and start to clean the ceiling with the same toothbrush. She's skinny with long curly red hair that is in a bun right now. When she's in a cleaning mood I have to stay on the couch so she can watch me and so I don't make a mess. Our house is tiny but open. There's no wall in between the kitchen and the living room, just a breakfast bar that sections it off and the change from carpet to tile. The front door is at the end of the kitchen and sits right next to our bathroom. I watch Mom walk along the counter and clean as much of the ceiling that she can reach. I pull my blanket on and eat a few more chips. This morning Mom gave me a bunch of snacks and a big water bottle so I wouldn't have to get up. But I have been here all day and I really have to pee.

Since the whole downstairs of our house is like one room, I can see through the kitchen and into the bathroom from the couch. I plan exactly where I'll step when I sneak to it. I jump off the couch and try take big steps so I don't get the floor dirty. I don't want Mom to be mad at me.

"What are you doing?" Mom yells. She jumps off the counter.

I freeze in the middle of making a big step. My legs are far apart and I say, "I have to pee."

Mom rolls her eyes and picks me up. She holds me a little too tight, and it's hard to breathe because she smells funny, almost like when I left my Barbie on the fireplace and she melted. The burnt plastic aroma lingers on her skin for days as she sweats out the meth in her system.

"It took me all morning to get the carpet strands to face the same way, I can't have you walking all over it!" She carries me to the bathroom and sets me down right next to the toilet. After going and washing my hands I tiptoe back to the couch. Mom follows me and brushes the tan carpet strands back in line after I walk on them.

"Don't touch anything else. I have to go and re-mop the floor now" Mom says as she hands me the remote.

I flip through a few channels while she crawls on all fours with a dirty rag mopping the already sparkling floor. Before I find Scooby Doo I hear something on the deck. The front door opens, and Dad walks in. He's tall and has white hair that he keeps short. He also has a white mustache that has just a little bit of brown in the center. I guess he used to have brown hair like me, before he got old. He says that 39 isn't old but I know he's old because of his hair.

"Where's my Mädchen?" He smiles at me. I wave at him as he walks through the kitchen and throws his dark green backpack onto the table in the living room. He plops down onto the couch with me, but before I can kiss him Mom starts to yell.

"Heinrich, I just cleaned the floor and you walk all over it. Now I have to do it all over again!" She's standing with her hands on her hips. That means she's mad.

"I didn't even make a mark, Natalie," He shows her the bottoms of his tennis shoes, "I don't have anything on my shoes." Pulling me close, he kisses my face. His face has a couple days' worth of growth on it and the whiskers are itchy and they tickle. I know he's rubbing them all over my face on purpose. After I push his face away, he scratches my back. It feels good.

"I don't care. The floor is dirty now," She stands up and pulls on the bottom of her shirt. It's one of Dad's old shirts and because he's so tall and strong it hangs off of her thin frame. "You're not going to get down on your hands and knees and scrub it are you?" Mom shoves pieces of her curly hair out of her face. Her bun is coming undone.

"You need to calm down. What's wrong with you?" Dad stops scratching my back and faces her, "It's a floor, people walk on it."

"Then you clean it." She throws the toothbrush at him. It bounces off his cheek and lands next to the vacuum.

"Thanks for welcoming me home. This is going to be a fucking fantastic day isn't it, Natalie?" He stands up, walks through the house, and out the door. It slams. Whenever Dad's mad he likes to take a walk. He says it's good for you to do that. Before I pick up my water bottle from where it fell, Mom runs to me. I try to squirm out of her arms, but she holds me tight. "I'm watching T.V!" I yell.

"Shut up," she hisses at me. She slips on her shoes and carries me outside. Even though it's still winter the trees are green and big. Most of the trees that make up the forest around us are evergreens like the Ponderosa Pine, Douglas-Fir, and Cedar. Because these trees grow so large, they cover most of the roadways in shade, which leaves them icy and treacherous to drive on in the winter. The cold mountain air makes me wish I had socks on. Mom sits in the driver's seat of the old VW bug and throws me into the seat next to her.

"I'm not getting your car seat, so you better hold on."

I smile. It's fun to break the rules. I hold onto the door and try to look out my window. Before we drive away, Dad comes around the corner of the house. He's yelling. I can't hear what he's saying though, because we're already flying down the road.

Mom doesn't stop at the stop sign at the top of the road near our house. I stand onto my seat so that I can see outside of the window. The car goes faster when we go down the steep hill next to Lake Gregory. The left side of the road leads to a deep ravine where trash and rocks pool after mudslides. Although the mountain communities are beautiful, they had to be built on the side of the mountain itself with the houses almost literally on top of one another. Many of them are built partially on stilts and make me queasy just looking at them. The streets are windy and narrow and often have hairpin turns with hidden driveways. Even the main roads are steep and will often parallel a ditch or ravine.

The fast turns and bumpy road make me feel sick. I roll down my window and breathe the cold air that smells just like

Christmas trees. As Mom turns onto a new street the wind pushes me against my seat. I feel like I'm flying over the lake. The water shimmers and is bright blue. It's always my favorite thing to drive past because it always seems so calm.

"Tara, sit your ass down. Your dad's following us."

I turn around and look behind us just as Mom speeds up. It's hard to stay standing but I want to see him. I hold on tight. When he gets close, I wave and smile. Mom turns into the neighborhoods where the big houses are. We make so many turns my stomach hurts. I face the front of the car again so I can see where we're going. Maybe then my stomach won't hurt.

Despite the wealthier houses being built here, the roads get skinny and bumpy the higher we go into the neighborhood. I hold onto the seat and swivel to check if Dad is still following us. I can just barely see the front of his car.

"He's still behind us," I say to Mom, not knowing that that was something she didn't want. She yells and turns onto a tiny dirt street. I slide sideways and Mom grabs me. My head sticks out of the window and I see Dad turn onto the same street. It's like playing chase. I guess Dad is 'it'. I laugh when Mom goes faster, not realizing that this is not a simple game of chase. The wind is strong, and it pulls my hair out of the window. It flaps around like a flag in a storm.

Mom pushes me down into the seat. "Hold on, I'm about to lose him."

I hope we don't lose Dad. I lost my favorite truck and I don't get to play with it anymore. Dad says that when you lose something it's gone forever. I hold onto the seat, tight, and rub the tears out of my eyes.

Mom makes the car go even faster. I try to watch the trees but they're moving too fast and it hurts my eyes. Instead I look at Mom. Her eyes are wide and her hair flies around her face.

The way she keeps look around her shoulder makes me nervous. Mom has never looked like this before, and it scares me. I hope dad will be able to catch us soon.

Mom soars around a big turn, hits a bump, and I fly. I hit the roof and land back in my seat. My head feels like it has exploded. It is hot and aches. I rub it until I feel like I might throw up. I can't see because my eyes are full of tears. Everything is blurry as I start to cry. We turn around another bend and Mom laughs.

"I told you I'd lose him." She looks over at me. Her thin face is covered in sweat despite the cold mountain air. "What's wrong with you?"

"I hit my head."

"I told you to hold on." She rubs my head, but her nails are long, and they scratch me a little each time she moves them. Pulling away, I smack her hand. Dad's lost and my head hurts and I just want to go home. I don't want to play chase anymore.

"Why don't you buckle up with the big buckle?" She scratches her face and I notice a little sore on her chin start to bleed.

"I can't get it. It's too hard to pull on."

"Oh well, we're almost there." She slams her foot down on the pedal.

After a few more turns Mom parks the car right next to big bush. We climb through the branches to get out. The little red berries tickle a little when I brush past them. I wonder if they are tasty or they will make me sick. We pile leaves and sticks over the back of the car to hide it. I don't know why we're hiding the car. Maybe it's another game mom and dad are playing. I wonder if Dad will be able to find us. After the car is covered, Mom carries me down the road.

The big yellow house she walks towards is dirty outside. There's trash all over the driveway and it looks like a skunk or raccoon got into it. I look around trying to spot the little animal. I love the white strip of fur on the stinktier's tail. I also really like the little black circles around the racoon's eyes. It reminds me of a bandit's mask. I can't see any before Mom is in front of the door. Mom knocks and whispers through the crack before we're let in. A lady with blonde hair makes us follow her into the dark living room.

"Leave her there. We'll go into my bedroom." Her voice is scratchy and sounds like she might be sick.

Mom puts me down in a big circle chair. It's like a bowl because it sinks in the middle and is filled with a big cushion that I lay on. Before leaving, Mom turns the T.V on and hands me my bottle.

I look around the house and see more trash. I can hardly see the floors and the walls even look dirty. The light on the TV is the only one on but it doesn't help me see into the dark corners. I try not to think of what might be crawling under all the trash. I tuck my toes under my butt, so they stay warm, and try to find a cartoon to watch.

Just when I'm about to fall asleep Mom comes back. She looks happy and smiles at me.

"Are we going home?" I ask.

"No, I'm just checking on you. Go to sleep." She covers me with a blanket and kneels on the floor next to my chair.

"Mom, you stink. Did you get sprayed by a stinktier?"

She laughs and rubs her hands on her jeans. "No, I didn't get sprayed by a skunk. Just go to sleep."

"But you smell like one. Does one live here? Can I see him?" I think about all the trash scattered around and I know a skunk must live here. Why else would it be so dirty?

She stops smiling. I notice that her eyes are extra big and think they look funny. "Tara, there is no skunk. Go to bed now."

She twirls my hair between her fingers and starts to sing. "Kookaburra sits in the old gum tree. Merry, merry king of the bush is he. Laugh, kookaburra. Laugh, kookaburra! Gay your life must be."

She normally doesn't do this. I feel safe and wish she would just crawl into the chair with me. Her hands are warm and feel so good that I feel myself falling asleep despite the weird smell on her fingers.

Someone is pounding on the door. It sounds like Dad and he's yelling. Mom runs out of a back room and covers my mouth.

"Don't say anything," she whispers with her stinky breath.

I squirm and the desperate need for my dad makes my eyes fill with tears. Mom's hand smells funny still. I don't like it over my mouth because it makes it hard to breath. I hope it doesn't give me an asthma attack. I don't think Mom has my inhaler with her. I wiggle away from her, trying to get some fresh air.

"Don't move!" She pins me down.

I try to yell for Dad but I can't get any words out with Mom on top of me. After a few minutes the house is quiet. Mom looks out of a window then runs to the back room and I can hear her talking. She runs back and looks at me. Her eyes are wide and she looks scared. I will see this look again and again over the course of my life and come to know that it means she is high. Really high on a mixture of her favorite drugs.

"Come on, Tara. We're leaving. But you have to be really quiet ok?" She wobbles a little, even though she is standing still. She regains her balance, picks me up, and sneaks through the door. Her feet crunch on the trash and other things left scattered everywhere. She runs to the car and starts tearing off the branches. I stand in the dirt, wiggling my toes, waiting for her. I make my toes dig little grooves into the ground and pretend they are little horses. Maybe if I keep them moving, they will warm up a little.

Just as Mom tears off the last branch Dad drives up and parks behind us so we can't leave. I try to run to him but Mom grabs me and holds me tight against her. I feel like my stomach is going to explode. Dad leaves his car on and jumps out.

"Are you out of your fucking mind?" He tears me out of her arms and hugs me. I wrap my arms around his neck. He smells like his insulin shots. He has to take them three times a day because he is type one diabetic. It smells strong and always stays on his shirts and the blankets. I like it. I'm happy he isn't lost.

"She just turned fucking four years old. How dare you drive around like a maniac with my daughter in the front seat! You didn't even buckle her up for Christ's sake. What the hell are you on?" He rubs my back and holds me tight. Not tight like Mom, but snuggly tight.

"Nothing," Mom's crying.

"Bullshit. You reek. You've been cleaning like you're on speed and chasing after drugs all week, haven't you?" He buckles me into my car seat and slams the door.

"No, I just didn't want to be around you!" she screams.

"Don't come home tonight," he takes off his jacket and covers me with it, making sure to tuck it under my bare toes. "You know what Natalie? Don't come home at all." He climbs into the driver's seat and locks the doors. I look out the window, but Mom is partially covered up by Dad's face and I can't really see her anymore.

To War

Dad slams the front door open so hard that it hits the wall with a loud pop. I slink down in my blanket and pretend I'm asleep.

"You're not even going to help me with my bags?" Mom screams from outside.

"I'm not fucking helping you with a single thing."

I know to stay still, especially if Dad is cussing. It means he's mad and I don't want him to know that I'm awake so early. Mom throws some bags onto the floor and slams the door shut.

"You're such a fucking gentleman," she says.

"Waking up at two in the morning to drive down to the airport to pick your sorry ass up isn't gentlemanly? Or me not leaving you there after seeing your neck covered in fucking hickeys? Or what about driving hours home, to our children, with you in the car knowing what you did?"

"They are not hickeys." She slams a cup of water onto the counter, "I told you that Jake pinched me."

"No way did your brother pinch you hard enough to leave three bruises on your neck. I was married for ten years before you and I screwed a lot of women before that. I know what a hickey looks like."

"They are *not* hickeys." Her voice is loud and low.

I roll over and peek out of my blanket. Dad turns to look at me and shakes his head.

"Shut up, Natalie. Tara's awake and I don't need her knowing that you're a slut, alright?"

"I'm not a slut! It's not a fucking hickey."

"Bullshit."

He turns and sits down on the floor next to me.

"Tara, do you know what day it is?" He smiles.

"Saturday?" I ask nervously.

"What do we do on Saturday?" he asks.

I look at his face for a minute, thinking. His eyes are red and he looks tired. He always looks tired because he works and goes to school so much. His smile is awkward, and I don't know why. Eventually I will learn to spot his forced smile. I will learn that it means he is unhappy, but too tired to keep fighting with mom. It is the face of someone who has given up. But this morning all I see is the face of my captain.

"We go to war!" I scream and jump out of my blankets. I run upstairs to get my gear on. In my sisters' room I have a dresser all to myself. I pull out some clothes and throw my pajamas onto the floor. Before running downstairs, I brush my hair with Emma's hairbrush and toss it back on her bed where she is still sleeping.

I race back downstairs and find Dad sitting on the deck outside. He points to the car and I beat him to it. I climb into the front seat of the old VW Bug. It doesn't matter that I can't see over the dash board or that my feet dangle inches above the floor. Dad is here. Everything is perfect.

"Are you ready soldier?" Dad yells as he climbs into our tank. He is tall and even with the seat all the way back, his legs bend funny. He looks a little bit like a cricket ready to jump.

I nod and smile. I buckle myself up and look at him waiting for the car to start.

"I can't hear you soldier. I asked if you are ready?" He looks at me, smiling.

"Yes Sir, Captain Daddy!" I bounce with excitement. War is my favorite game.

"Who is the target today?" Captain Daddy asks me as we make our way to the battle.

"The bad guys, Sir!" I yell as I fidget in my seat.

"Correct. What are we going to do to the scum bags?" His deep voice is loud and curt like all the men in the war movies we watch.

"We're going to squish them!" I slam my fist into my hand and search his face for approval.

"Yes we are. Get ready." He smiles and puts the car into gear. As we drive towards the battle I get nervous. I hope we win.

The green-blue water of Lake Gregory comes into view. The manmade lake was built as a damn back in the 1930's. It is said that one day, towards the end of the project, it started to rain. It rained for three straight days and filled the lake up so much that the men building it left all sorts of equipment at the bottom. I always hope I will be able to see a tractor in the water one day. But today the only thing I see is our battlefield and its surroundings. We finally make it to the battle. I kneel on the seat so that I can see out of the tank's window.

"Soldier, how does it look out there? I need a full report." Dad points through the window to the two-lane mountain road.

I gaze out the window. The light coming from the glittering water blinds me for a minute. "Captain Daddy, there are a few other tanks coming for us. There's also some bad guys running around." I point to the few cars slowly driving towards us and the early morning joggers.

"Load the weapon with the missile." He pats the dashboard of the car and slows down.

"Is a missile like a torpedo? Can we use torpedoes like in the submarine movie we watched yesterday?"

"Sure. Get a torpedo and get ready to fire!"

I reach back for my imaginary squad to hand me the torpedo. It's heavy and dark green. I can barely lift it. I struggle to open the glove compartment where our weapon is stored.

"Careful soldier, don't blow us to smithereens!" He reaches over and helps me load the weapon. With his help it goes safely into our gun. Once it's snug, I close the compartment and wait.

"Pick your target," Dad glances at me from the side.

"We should take out the other tanks first…right Captain?" I ask. In all the World War Two movies we watch, the tanks always try to fire on other tanks first. I guess it is best to destroy the thing that could hurt you. After the enemy tanks are all taken care of, the tanks fire on everything else too like buildings and people.

"That's a good idea. One day you're going to be Captain." He smiles and pushes my hair out of my face.

I aim for the closest tank. It's a yellow minivan with a bent bumper. It should go down easily.

"Straight ahead Captain, the yellow one."

He nods and slows down even more.

"Ready…aim…FIRE!" He screams.

I hit the glove compartments button. It pops open and the torpedo is on its way. It whistles while it flies through the air. Finally, it hits its target. The BOOM makes our tank shake.

"Target destroyed. Good work soldier."

"Thanks Daddy. Can we do another?" I begin to scan the area for other enemies. The lake is surrounded by pine trees and mountain peaks. A rowboat floats along in the middle of

it with a lone fisherman inside. Through the trees, rooftops and bits of homes peak out. Along the shore there is a small path that people like to use to run or walk when the weather is nice.

"Duh, the battle isn't over. Get another torpedo!"

I scramble for another torpedo. This one takes out a fat woman bad guy who is running by the lake. The next one takes out a blue tank. Pieces of the metal fly in all directions. Dad stops me while I load another.

"We're arriving at our destination. Do you remember our goal?" He turns to me while turning off the car.

"We have to get food for breakfast and paper for our butts." I count the two things on my hand and hope I didn't forget anything.

"And...?" His question stops my heart.

I can't remember what else we need. I stare into his face searching for clues. But nothing comes to mind. I slump in my seat and stare at my shoes. The ugly sandals are hand-me-downs from my sister. I hate wearing them but I know that money is tight. I wiggle my toes and try not to cry.

"Teester, don't cry. We need *milch* remember?"

Milk! How could I have forgotten milk?

"Sorry Dad."

"It's ok. Let's go." He gets out and helps me climb down. He has to slam the door before it shuts all the way. We've always had to do that on the right side of the car. I hold Dad's hand as we go into Goodwin's Market. The floor is white and the isles tower over me. I always feel like I'm going to get lost. I keep close to Dad. We find the bacon, eggs and milk in the back where it's cold. Dad pulls me to the front.

I yank on his hand, "Don't forget the butt paper!"

"I almost forgot. Good thing I have you." He ruffles my hair and pulls me along the long isle. I beam. Once we grab the toilet paper we're on our way to the ladies in the front. There is no line for us to wait in. I guess people don't like waking up early on Saturdays. I don't know why. They're the best day because Dad's here.

"Henry, she's gotten so big! How old is she now? It feels like I've been away so long," the cashier says. Her red lips smile at me. After pushing some buttons she stares down at me and waits. I don't like it. I grab Dad's leg and hide my face behind him.

"Tara, tell her how old you are." He reaches for me and tries to pull me off his leg. After several good tugs he gives up.

"She turned four about six months ago." He smiles at the woman and hands her the cash for our things.

"Well give her this for me as a birthday gift." I peak my head around and watch her put a piece of candy in the bag. Before she can look at me again, I hide.

"Thanks. See you around." Dad smiles and picks up the bag with my candy. He motions for me to follow him. I cling to his leg as we walk out of the sliding doors. Once we're in the car I dig through the bag and find my candy. It's a piece of my favorite chocolate. I tear it open and pass it to Dad. After he takes a small bite I shove the rest into my mouth and suck on it.

"Are you ready for round two of the battle?" He tickles me until I can't breathe.

"Yes, Captain," I wheeze.

"Let's go to war."

We drive back home and destroy a few more bad guys on the way. When Dad parks he hands me the eggs and bacon to carry upstairs. The stairs he made from dirt and wood railroad ties wrap around the left side of the house and lead to the big deck. Dad says the deck is a party deck since it is so big. It stretches around to the front door. Dad lets us in and sets down his bags. Mom is in the bathroom, slamming things around.

Dad takes out a frying pan and has me hand him each piece of bacon after opening the package with a knife. They sizzle and get curly before he pulls them out and lays them on a plate with a bunch of paper towels on it. The salty smell makes my mouth water. He scratches his long nose with the end of his finger before flipping the next batch over.

Mom comes out of the bathroom and lets the door slam closed. She looks mad. She pushes me out of her way as she passes. I fall onto the ground and stay still. I don't want to give her a reason to push or hit me. She washes her hands in the kitchen sink without even looking at me. I stand up and stand close to dad.

"Don't shove your daughter." Dad's voice is calm, but he clenches his jaw.

"Shut up." Mom glares at him and pushes me again.

"Get out." Dad says, putting his spatula down and wiping his hands on a rag that is sticking out of his back pocket.

"Why don't you make me?" her eyes narrow and she pushes her chest up.

Dad takes his fingers and pokes her in the chest. He does it so hard that she stumbles backwards. "Don't ever push my daughter. Get the fuck out."

"Whatever, like I want to stay here with you." She shoves him as she walks past him.

"Just go back to Nebraska and screw around some more. That's all you're good at anyways." Dad pulls me close to him. Mom shows him her middle finger and goes outside. I hear the car start and speed off before Dad lets go of my shoulders.

"Did I make Mom mad?" I ask.

"No, T, you didn't do anything. She's just being dumb right now."

"I'm sorry Mom has some hickeys. I bet she didn't mean to get them. I never mean to get bruises."

He stares at me, silent, for a long time. "She did mean to get them. That's the problem," he brushes my hair behind my ear and sighs, "I don't want you to worry about it anymore."

"When she comes home are you going to fight more?"

"No, we won't. I promise. Why don't you go get Emma up for breakfast?"

I wipe my hands on his rag too and run upstairs.

To the left of the stairs is dad's study closet. I think it was meant to be an actual closet but dad was able to fit a tiny desk in there. He uses it to write his school papers and study. It's piled high with books and loose sheets of paper. I like to sneak up here during the day and look at his books. I want to know what they mean. I check Dad's study closet first, but I know I won't find Emma in there. She hates to read. I look into the big room on the right-hand side of the stairs. It's the only actual bedroom in the house. Mom filled it with a huge bed for her and Emma to share. I don't mind that they get the bed though. Every night Dad gets out the huge army sleeping bag and a few blankets and lays them on the floor in the living room. We use the couch cushions as pillows and get to watch our war movies together that way. I love it.

I see Emma's feet move around for a minute in the bed. I try shaking her, but she just punches me and rolls over. I run back down the stairs and jump the last few.

"She doesn't want to get up," I say, picking up the eggs in their shells and handing them to him.

"Well, I guess it's just you and me."

He cracks an egg, lets it cook a little and then flips it over. Before it cooks all the way he puts in on my plate and sends me into the living room. He comes and sits next to me and we share a glass of milk.

"You want to finish the World War Two show we started last night?" He asks.

"Yeah!" I got to see parts of Germany where Dad is from and even hear how they speak there. Dad even taught me some German words, like *milch* which is milk and *stinktier* that is skunk. I like saying those words. They sound funny.

"Let's see how the war ended then, alright?" he grabs the remote and turns the movie back on. I take a big bite of bacon covered in the yoke of the egg and watch a real tank shoot down a jeep from across town. The screen flashes to a little girl standing in rubble all by herself. I wonder where her dad is and if they ever get to see each other again. The screen changes again to aerial views of Germany. I don't know how anyone will be able to rebuild after the unimaginable destruction. Maybe, somehow, the city will rise out of the ashes better than it was before.

I settle down next to dad and take a deep breath. War movies always make me feel better after a battle was fought in the house.

10 Weeks

Our new cabin is filled with boxes, but the only one I care about is an old long box labeled "Alex's Tree". I pull it out from under a few trash bags full of clothes and open the top. A small Christmas tree is folded inside and must only stand at a few feet tall. It's perfect for our first Christmas tree.

"You need help moving the boxes around?" Alex asks, coming in from the one bedroom where he has been putting together our bed.

"No, I'm fine."

"Just don't overdo it." He smiles and looks at my stomach. I know he must be thinking about the twins. I turn my back to him and hide my tiny belly. It looks more like I had a big lunch than having two babies in there. Guilt washes over me as I pull on the tree. I know I should be more excited about the pregnancy. To be honest, when I think about the two tiny babies and how cute they will be I can't wait to hold them. I know that I will love them immensely. I'm just not sure if I'll do a good job with everything.

"I won't over do it. Promise." I lay the Christmas tree onto the counter that separates the living room and the kitchen. It's almost like a breakfast bar and is the best place to set up the tree. I will be able to see it from anywhere in our house from there.

"Why is your name on the box?" I ask, setting up the base.

Alex rummages around inside of a box on the kitchen floor and pulls out a glass, "It used to be the one I set up in my room when I was little." He fills the glass with water from the tap and drains it in one drink.

I lay a red blanket down on the counter and set the base right in the middle. "So, you didn't have a family tree? You just set one up in your room?"

I place the tree on top of the base. The branches are still crumpled and need fluffing out, but I'm excited to see the tree up. Our cabin is looking a little more like a home.

"No, we had a family tree, too. We just each got our own little one that we could decorate however we wanted." Alex starts to spread the branches out. As he works on one side, I work on the other.

"How'd you decorate it?" I ask.

Alex stretches the top of the tree out. "Mom would buy us each an ornament every Christmas just for our tree. I had soccer ones and snowmen and a Santa one."

I take a big plastic cylinder out of a target bag near my feet. It's filled with little plastic balls. They're red, gold and silver and all about the same size. It was on sale and I thought the colors looked nice together. I open it and start to pull out the new ornaments.

"Where's your old Christmas box?" Alex asks me.

I look into the living room where towers of boxes makes the room look even smaller than it actually is. I tried to keep it organized, but Alex wouldn't let me lift anything. I know he is trying to be helpful and make sure the babies are alright, but just because I'm pregnant doesn't mean I can't do anything. I take a deep breath and try to let the irritation fade away by focusing on how caring he is being. "Uh, maybe by the door?"

I point to the side door that has a glass panel in the middle. Light streams in and it looks beautiful, but tonight we will have to tape something up to block it. I don't want anyone looking in through the glass at night.

Alex walks to the door and pushes a few boxes around. He pulls a small box out from the bottom of a stack. "Is this it?" He holds it up, "It's pretty small."

I look up and nod. "It doesn't have that much in there."

He brings it over to me and lays it on the table. It's only about the size of a few tissue boxes stacked on top of each other. I rip the tape off the top and peer inside. Old newspaper covers most of the contents. I pull the top layer off and see the red and white stocking on top. It's old and soft. I lay it down on the counter and pull out a ball of newspaper.

I pull the corner of the paper and unravel it. Underneath all the layers is an old bumble bee ornament. It's ceramic and has a few tiny cracks. The yellow and black paint is chipping off so I hold it carefully. I rub my finger around the edge of the wings and close my eyes. I can almost feel cold winter air in my face and smell the hint of apple shampoo.

"What's that?" Alex's voice pulls me back into my living room. I open my eyes and hold up the ornament.

"It's just an old ornament. It's cracked and chipping though, so I think I'm just going to toss it." I set it down on the counter and continue to unwrap a few other ornaments. I place each on the tree.

His eyebrows furrow. "But that's from Santa's Village." His tone implies the importance, but I just shrug.

"Yeah, but it's old and I want to get new ones. I want our tree to be just ours, with ornaments that we get. Not left overs."

"You're being a little dramatic." He walks over to me and pulls me into a hug.

"No, I'm not." I let him give me a kiss on the forehead, but then pull away. He walks back into the bedroom to finish setting up the bed.

I stare at the ornament on the white counter. It's one of my favorite things from my childhood. I wonder if Alex is right. He has an annoying habit of knowing me too well, and is generally right when he gives me advice.

I turn over the ornament and see a little heart etched into the back. It's from Mom. I rewrap it in the newspaper and place it back in the box. I press my hand on my stomach. Just under the surface I feel a little something move against my palm. I pull my hand off my stomach quickly, almost revolted. I remind myself that I'm only 10 weeks along. It's way too early to feel the babies move. It must have just been my imagination.

Trolls and Knights

I'm sitting on the dirty living room carpet when Mom leaves us home alone, again. After fighting with Dad so much, Mom took my sister, Emma, and me and we moved into a different house a few months ago. We don't get to see Dad that much unless he's giving us money for food or bringing us some more clothes. I don't know where Mom goes all the time since she doesn't have a job, but I know that I will get in trouble if I ask. Hopefully she will be home soon.

The new house we live in is behind the bowling alley on a little dirt road. I like to call the new house 'The Hole' because Dad always says it's a shit hole, but I'm not allowed to say the first word. The house is tiny and dirty. It always has a strange smell that must be related to how old it is or how it doesn't get cleaned very much.

The neighborhood is filled with trash and loose dogs. Even being so close to the main street of Crestline, this area is plagued with drugs, violence and the impoverished. Our house is no exception. It has a lot of broken windows that we fix with tape. The paint is peeling off the walls, but Mom doesn't want to fix it. She says that it isn't her job to do it. There is a big bedroom upstairs that Mom and Emma share. Downstairs there is the living room, bathroom, kitchen and my room. My bedroom has two big windows that are cracked so at night I use Dad's sleeping bag to stay warm. He brought it to me a few weeks ago. That's the last time I saw him.

"You want some Mac and Cheese?" Emma asks from inside the kitchen. I sniff the air and can tell that she burnt it. I'm so hungry that I don't care.

"Yeah!" I jump up from the floor and find her in the kitchen. The kitchen has no lights, so it's always dark. It has just enough room for our refrigerator that leaks water, a small stove and the kitchen sink. Emma is standing by the stove stirring a pot. Her red hair is curly like mom's and falls down to her butt. She is tall and skinny and has green eyes like Mom too. I wish I looked like them a little. Instead of curly, I have straight hair and it's dark brown. My blue eyes are just like Dad's which always makes Mom mad. I guess she doesn't like to be reminded of him. Especially now that they broke up. Emma looks at me and motions for me to get a bowl.

I look for some bowls and forks, in the one cupboard above the sink, but there are none. Emma just takes the whole pot into the living room. We share the wooden spoon and take turns eating a few bites at a time. The cheese is clumpy, and the noodles are still pretty hard, but Emma is only nine, so I don't tell her how gross it is. I'm just happy to have some warm food.

"When is Mom coming home?" I ask while Emma takes a few bites.

"Soon, I think." She takes another big bite and passes me the spoon.

I take a few bites of crunchy noodles and smile.

"What are you smiling about?"

"The noodles are crunchy…" I try not to laugh, but I can't help it. I spit chunks of noodles out while I laugh on accident.

A few pieces land on Emma. It makes me laugh harder. "It's pretty bad," she says, pushing the noodles around the pot.

"Maybe Dad can bring over something for dinner. Maybe Mom can call him?" I ask. I miss Dad so much.

"Dad's not coming back. Get used to it. My real dad lives in Nebraska and doesn't ever call. Your dad's going to do the same." She glares at me. Normally she doesn't mention her real father. All I know about him is that he got mom pregnant when she was sixteen and left soon after Emma was born. He never calls her or even sends her a birthday card. I guess she doesn't like to think about him that much since he never spends time with her. Dad told me that Emma is actually his daughter since he raised her from when she was only a year old. He always tells me to call her my sister, even though she calls me her half-sister.

"No, he'll come back. He said he would always come back for me." It feels like I just swallowed a big lump of noodles. I miss the smell of his insulin. The smell always stays on his shirts and when I snuggle him I like to sniff it because there is nothing else like it in the whole world. I also miss when he would let me crawl into his lap and he would scratch my back. He would use his nails and scratch just hard enough to feel good and at the very end he would make his hands go so fast I felt like I was going to fly out of his lap. I also miss helping him do his research in his big books and watching shows with him. I miss just being around him.

She rolls her eyes. "You're four and a half now, stop being such a baby." She finishes the food before going back into the kitchen. I look around the living room and try to forget about what she said. The room is pretty empty except one small couch and a box of toys. The old TV with a VCR attached to it sits on the floor across from the couch. The rest of the room is just a path that we have to keep clean so that we can walk to the rest of the rooms.

I dig around in the box of toys and find the stuffed animal stinktier that Dad gave me. He is as long as my arm, black with a white stripe down his back. My favorite part is the little rough patch of fur on the top of his head. I like to brush it so it sticks up in a line. I named him Stinky, since skunks smell so bad. I hold him tight. Dad will come back. He said he would never leave me alone and that he will visit soon. I know he will come back and hopefully he will take us all home. I miss seeing him every day and sleeping next to him at night. Mom makes fun of me for that. When we were still at home with dad, Mom said that since I'm four and a half I should sleep upstairs on the floor in Emma's room. But when Dad lays out our sleeping blankets on the floor in the living room and turns on a history movie, I don't ever want to move. I like having him close to me, I know I'm safe.

"He's going to take us home soon, Stinky." I whisper to the skunk as I give him a hug. I plop down onto the couch, cover us both up with a blanket, and try to believe in my own words.

Emma coms back in and sits down next to me. "Mom's outside. She seems upset."

Before I can look out of the window, the door flies open and slams against the wall, leaving a big dent where the doorknob hits.

"Why is it so cold in here?" She slams the front door and stomps to the heater. She hits the dial a few times and it clicks but doesn't turn on.

"Piece of shit." Mom hits it again, but it doesn't do anything.

"You ok, Mom?" I ask.

She turns to me and stares at me. Her green eyes are red and puffy, and her curly hair is pretty messy. It looks like she was in a fight with someone.

"I'm fine Tara. Why don't you watch a movie?" She goes upstairs and slams that door too.

"You shouldn't ask her anything, idiot. Now she's mad at us." Emma digs around the toy box and pulls out a few VHS' that Dad dropped off a while ago. She puts one in and turns the TV up. Before the movie even starts Mom comes back downstairs.

She's wearing tight black pants and a silky red top. She drags some dark red lipstick across her lips before throwing it back up the stairs.

"I'm going to go see your Dad for a few minutes and then I'm going to go visit a friend. Joe is going to come watch you for a few hours, alright?"

Emma just nods her head.

"Who's Joe?" I ask.

"He's a friend of mine. Be nice to him and do what he says." Mom runs her fingers through her hair and scrunches it up a few times letting the curls bounce up and down.

"Can I go see Dad with you?" I squeeze Stinky and make a wish that she says yes.

"No, you have to stay here."

"But I want to see him! I promise I'll be good."

She glares at me. "I said no."

"But I want to see Dad!" I yell.

"I don't have time for you. Go to your room until I leave." She grabs my shoulder so I'm standing and shoves me towards my room.

"I hate you!" I scream and run into my room. I slam the door, just like she did, and jump into bed. Crawling into bed is not what I want to be doing. Why cant things go back to normal? I snuggle into Dad's sleeping bag and when I smell his insulin I start to cry. I hate Mom for taking me away from

Dad. I hate her for not letting me see him and always leaving us alone.

A little while later I hear the door open and close. I hope Dad is nice to Mom when they see each other. Then maybe she will let us go back home.

"Tara?" a man calls out from behind my door. He knocks once and then opens it. I poke my head out of my sleeping bag and watch him come into my room. He is short and has an enormous belly. His blonde hair has large bald spots that he has tried to hide by combing over the rest of his thin strands. It all kind of sticks up funny and makes it look worse. I've never seen him before.

"My name's Joe. Why don't you come out and watch a movie with us?" He holds out his hand to me. It's greasy and shakes.

"No." I say. I don't want to be anywhere near him. He smells weird and I don't like the way he smiles at me.

"Come on, you have to listen to me. Your mom left me in charge." He smiles and I can see all of his teeth. He has a few golden ones and they shine in the light. "When she comes home I don't want to have to tell her that you didn't listen to me."

I wrap the sleeping bag around me tight and jump like a bunny out of my room and into the living room. Emma is on the couch watching a movie. She pats the couch next to her for me to sit. Normally, she doesn't want me anywhere near her, but I guess because Joe is here, she wants me close. I lay on the couch next to Emma and she spreads out too, so we fill the entire thing. When I lay my head too close to her she pushes me away a little. I guess she wants me close, but not too close. I watch Joe come into the room and watch us for a while. Every time I look at him he looks at the TV.

"Tara, why don't you sit on my lap so we can all be on the couch together?" He sits on the arm rest, next to my feet.

I pretend that I don't hear him. I don't want to sit on his lap. I don't know why he would even ask. It reminds me of when Dad always says to run away from strangers or hit them if they want to touch me. He said that there are bad men that will do bad things to little girls and that I should always run away from them.

But Joe is our babysitter. Mom must be good friends with him to have him watch us. I wonder if he is just a nice person. I peer up at his face and see him watching me again. He smiles and pats his legs like Santa does around Christmas time in the mall. I glare at him and kick him off the edge of the couch.

"You are going to get a spanking if you keep acting like that." He stands up and rubs the front of his pants near his zipper.

"You won't touch her or I'll tell our Dad." Emma says, without looking at him.

His eyes grow wide and he mumbles as he walks into the kitchen.

"You think Dad will come back if we call him?" I ask.

"We don't have a phone, stupid" She looks at me over her shoulder before turning away, "It got shut off yesterday." Her voice is low and she looks nervous as she watches the kitchen doorway for any signs of Joe.

"Maybe we could walk to Goodwin's and call him from there?" I scoot next to her and this time she doesn't push me away. I don't quite understand why we are suddenly on the same side, but I feel better knowing she is here with me.

The market is down the road and I bet the ladies who work the cashier counters would let us use the phone. They are always so nice when I go shopping with Dad.

"I don't want to leave. If Mom comes home and we aren't here we will get in so much trouble."

"What do you want to do then?" I ask.

"Let's just keep him away from us," she bites her lip in thought.

I dig around in my sleeping bag until I find Stinky. I hug him and watch the movie.

Emma elbows me in the side after a while. I almost yell at her, but when I see her face I stay quite. Her green eyes are big and she looks afraid.

"What?" I whisper.

She looks around the house and grabs my hand. She stands up and pulls me after her towards the bathroom. When we hear a noise from my bedroom we run into the bathroom. Emma carefully closes the door and locks it. I wiggle my toes on the cold blue tile and smile up at her.

"We made it!" I whisper.

"Shut up!" she says.

She leans against the door and presses her ear against it. I hold my breath and rub the side of the sink. The bathroom is small, like everything else in the house, but at least it has a bathtub in it. It's jammed right next to the toilet and sink. That's all that fits in the room. There is barely enough room for us to stand next to each other.

I wait for Emma to do something. She just stands there. After what must have been an hour she turns to me with her finger on her lips. She doesn't want me to make a sound. She backs away from the door and pushes me almost into the bathtub. Just as my legs hit the rim, the doorknob jingles and clicks. It sounds like someone is trying to unlock it.

"Turn the bath on," Emma says, "I'm going to call Dad." Her voice is loud.

"On what?" I whisper.

"I'm *pretending* so maybe Joe will leave us alone." She whispers so quietly that I have to watch her lips move to understand what she is saying.

I think about Dad and how strong he is while I turn the warm water on. I bet he could kill a person just by hitting them. I guess Emma knows this too, and even though she calls him her fake Dad when she's mad, she knows he will protect her just like a real Dad does.

"Hey, Dad!" Emma's voice is a little too loud, but the jingling doorknob stops moving, "Oh yeah we're just about to take a bath." She waits for a few seconds. I smile at her. "Yeah Joe's watching us. He's a little weird." She says the last part louder.

There is a noise outside of the door and it sounds like Joe is pushing on it. I hope he doesn't get in.

"Oh yeah, I'll tell him that you'll come meet him later," she says towards the door.

"You think Joe believes you?" I whisper.

Emma smacks my arm and gives me a dirty look. "Yeah, I'll see you in a little while Dad," She says, turning back towards the door, "Love you. Bye," she says before slamming her hand on the counter. She smiles at me and I have to put my hand over my mouth to keep from giggling. I hope Joe believes Emma's fake phone call. Hopefully Dad will actually come over after he visits with Mom. Then he will protect us from Joe. I don't know why I want protection from Joe. I don't know what a pedophile is let alone understand anything that deals with sex. All I know is that deep down something tells me that Joe is not someone I want to be around.

Emma pulls off her socks one at a time. "Let's get in the tub and try to stay in as long as we can. We can even refill it with hot water once it gets cold."

I pull off my shirt and toss it on the floor. I love warm baths. I throw the rest of my clothes onto the shirt and jump in.

"Let's put bubbles in it!" I say.

"Just use some of the shampoo," Emma says, climbing into the tub with me. Her voice is lower than normal and I wonder if she is still worried about Joe.

I squirt some shampoo right underneath the faucet and watch the bubbles fill the rest of the tub. I give myself a beard and some big bubble eyebrows. I try wiggling them, but they just fall off my face. Maybe I can make her laugh so that she isn't so worried anymore.

"You're such a weirdo!" Emma says, laughing at me.

"Girls?" Joe calls from behind the door.

I look at Emma and freeze. She puts her finger back to her lip and we both stay quiet.

Joe taps on the door a few times. "Girls, I don't think you should be in the bathroom alone. It's dangerous to take a bath without an adult." He tries the doorknob. "Why don't you let me in so I can make sure you're safe?" The doorknob turns slowly but doesn't open. He wiggles it frantically until it sounds like it is going to fall off.

I open my mouth to say something, but Emma shakes her head. I close my mouth again and sink deeper into the water until only my head is above the surface.

"Girls, I really need to be in there with you. Let me in." Joe's voice is louder and sounds more upset. Mom lets us take baths alone all the time. I know Joe doesn't need to be in here with us. I don't know why he would want to be anyways.

"Why does he want in?" I whisper to Emma.

"Because he's a creep."

"What does that mean?" I ask.

"It means he is a gross old guy who wants to see us naked." She whispers back. She scrubs her hair with shampoo and dunks under the water to rinse it out. I wonder how a nine year old know this, but at the time I just figure that she is older and must know more than I do.

"You know your mom left me in charge!" Joe yells from outside of the door.

I pull on Emma until her head pops back up, covered in bubbles. I slide next to her and point at the bottom of the door. We watch as Joe walks back and forth in front of our door, occasionally kicking it as he goes.

"You have to let me in!" He pounds on the door again.

"Joe, leave us alone or I will call our Dad again. He's not happy that a guy is watching us anyways," Emma yells.

I can hear Joe mumbling outside of the door before he walks away. The TV turns on and I relax a little in the water.

"If he tries that again, we are going to go to Goodwin's and call Dad." Emma looks just as scared as I feel.

"What if Joe doesn't let us out of the house?" I ask.

"We will just sneak out of the window in here if Mom isn't back soon." She puts some shampoo in my hair. I dunk under the water for a minute, but it's getting cold and I don't like to hold my breath that long. I put just my eyes and nose above the water and spit some at Emma. She splashes me back.

"Can we refill it with hot water again?" I ask.

"Yeah, unplug it."

I yank on the little chain in the bottom of the tub and watch the bubbles and water spiral out of the drain. Emma turns the water back on and I let it run over my hair for a few minutes before putting the plug back in and sitting up.

I hear footsteps again and turn towards the door. Emma points at the bottom and we see that Joe is back.

"You know what, if you don't let me in right now I am going to kick the door in." He says. His voice is calm. It scares me more than when he was yelling.

"If you kick the door in, my mom will be really mad." Emma says.

"She's going to be mad that you are in there alone. If I tell her how you weren't listening you'll both be in big trouble."

"I'll just tell her how creepy you are and she'll call the cops."

I can hear Joe cussing as he paces the hallway again. My hands are shaking and I don't know what to do.

"Get out, dry off and get dressed," Emma says, "But be quite."

I nod and jump out. Underneath the sink I find a few towels and dry off as fast as I can. I throw Emma my towel and start to get dressed. Emma wraps her hair up and tries to open the window that is above the bath. It opens with a screech.

"What are you girls doing in there?" Joe shakes the door and it really sounds like it is going to fall apart. "Let me in! I just want to make sure that you're clean and soaped all the right areas and rinsed off all the way. I'm worried about you." He calls from behind the door. He doesn't sound worried. He just sounds like her really wants in. I'm too young to know what lust sounds like, but years later I will remember this night and hate mom all over again for leaving us. Especially for leaving us with Joe. "Girls, please?" His voice is soft.

Emma throws me my socks and I pull them on. They're damp, but I don't say anything about it. Emma pull down her shirt just when I hear the front door open.

"It's got to be Dad!" I say, forgetting that we never actually called him and that he probably isn't coming over. I walk to the door and start to unlock it. Emma pulls me away and pushes me onto the floor before I open it.

"You're so dumb," she hisses, "Don't open it." She looks at the bottom of the door and raises her eyebrows. Joe's shadow is still there.

"Why?"

"It could be a trick from Joe. I'm not opening it until I hear Mom's voice." She pushes her ear to the door. I wonder how she knows these things. The fake phone call, the shadow under the door and not falling for any of his tricks are things I never even thought of. If I had been in charge we would probably never even have locked ourselves in the bathroom. Maybe she knows all the tricks because she fell for them once. Maybe this has happened before.

"Tara, Emma, come out here!" Mom yells. She sounds happy so I open the door and run to her. Her hair is kind of flattened and her clothes are wrinkly, but she smiles and gives me a hug.

"Dad gave me some groceries and a few toys for you guys. They're in the front seat of the bug, go get them." She smiles and points to the front door.

I run outside in my wet socks and open the car. The whole front seat is full of bags from Goodwin's and most of the back seat too. I look behind me and smile at Emma. Her eyes are wide, and she digs through the first bag looking for candy. Dad always sneaks us candy when he gives us food.

"Jackpot!" She says, pulling out a whole Payday and Snickers bar. She throws me the Payday and rips into her snickers wrapper.

"Dad must be happy since he sent us so much food!" I say, through a mouthful of candy.

"Yeah, maybe Mom did something nice for him."

I think about her pretty red shirt and how she even did her make up today. I bet dad thought she looked beautiful, so he gave us extra stuff. After finishing our candy, we drag the groceries inside the house. Mom puts them away and makes dinner for us. A huge baked potao, green beans, and roasted chicken fills up my entire plate. We haven't eaten like this since we moved. I eat two entire helpings, not knowing the next time I'll get a chance to eat like this. My stomach hurts and I feel like I'm about to explode, but I'm finally warm. After eating, Mom piles the plates into the sink and lays on the living room floor.

"Where's Joe?" I ask. I completely forgot about him.

"He went home. Was he nice?" she asks.

"No, he's a creeper who wanted us naked" I say.

"What?" She looks at me and I shrug. "Emma, what is Tara talking about?"

Emma takes a deep breath and tells her all about how Joe was during the night. Mom looks mad. She keeps shaking he head.

"That bastard!" She pulls me close and looks at me. "I'm so sorry I left you with him. I won't ever do that again." She kisses my forehead and I lean against her. I'm so sleepy after such a long day and a full belly that I can feel my eyes closing on her shoulder.

"Teester, why don't you go to bed? I'll tell you a story and then you can go to sleep, k?" She pulls me up and brings me into my room. It's cold and I can hear the wind whistling through the duct tape windows, but when she wraps me up in the sleeping bag I don't mind the noise so much.

I face the wall and windows, with my back towards the door so Mom can scratch it while she tells me a story. She talks about trolls and brave knights with swords and I can't keep my eyes open. I let them close and imagine what she is saying. When she stops talking I open my eyes.

In the window outside I see a face. I wonder if it is one of the trolls from her stories. It scares me. I scream.

"What?" Mom yells.

"The troll in the window!"

She looks out of my window and screams too. She runs to it and opens it. The screen is cut and flaps in the wind, but the face is gone.

Mom grabs me and drags me into the living room. "Don't move," she says, throwing me on the couch with Emma. Emma wraps her arms around me. Our rivalry has always kept a wall between us but in this moment, there is no space between us. All that matters is that we are sisters and that means we keep each other safe. Mom opens the front door and looks outside.

"You fucking bastard! Stay away from me and my kids!" She screams. The yard is quiet and dark. Emma pulls me close.

"Ask to go home," she whispers.

"What?" I say.

"Ask Mom to take us home with Dad. She'll do it now. Dad made her happy today and there was some man in your window. She'll take us home now," she whispers.

"Mom?" I call. Mom turns to me and comes back in the house. She closes the door and locks it.

"You ok?" She sits next to us on the couch.

"Can we go back home now?" I ask. "Please?" I start to cry without meaning to. I just miss Dad so much and I know he will keep us all safe.

Mom rubs my back and is quiet.

"Mom, please?" Emma asks.

"Yeah, I'll take you home. Go upstairs and pack your stuff. Tara, stay out of your room. I'll get your stuff." She leaves me sitting there and goes into my room. Emma runs upstairs, and I can hear things moving around.

I find Stinky sitting next to me and smile. "We're going home!" I say.

"I'll pack up the rest of our stuff tomorrow. Let's just get in the car." Mom yells up the stairs for Emma.

Emma comes downstairs with her backpack. Mom holds my hand and takes us to the car. After buckling up she drives through town and next to the lake. She pulls into the driveway and honks. I can't wait for Dad to come out. I run unbuckle and jump out. I race up the stairs, that Dad and I built last summer, and run onto the deck. Just when I'm about to reach the door Dad opens it.

His face is a mask of surprise when I jump into his arms. His smell and warmth are as familiar to me as his face. He wraps his strong arms around me and scratches my back just the way I like. He's like the knight in mom's stories- always ready to protect me.

"What are you doing here?" he asks. His voice sounds a little scratchy and he rubs his eyes a few times.

"We're coming back home!" I yell. His eyebrows go down and he looks upset.

"You want us home, right?" I ask, suddenly afraid that he hasn't missed me as much as I have missed him.

"I never wanted you to leave. I'm just," he pauses and looks out into the driveway, "Surprised, that's all."

I look into the driveway too, and see mom sitting on the roof of her car. Her smile fills her face and her green eyes seem to light up. She tosses her ringlet curls behind her shoulder and waves at us. She is the most beautiful person I have ever seen.

"We won't go away again, right Dad?" I ask.

"I'll never let your Mom take you away again. I'll do anything to keep her happy so that you can stay with me. Ich liebe dich, meine Prinzessin."

I hold him tight and he takes me inside. I never think about how hard it was for him to be without me. I never know how dangerous it really was living with Mom and Emma in the 'hole' until years later. When I'm searching for my own cabin I pass over the exact house without a doubt. The neighborhood is still run donw and my old bedroom window is still broken.

As I write this, I get chills thinking about how close we were to being sexually abused by a pedophile. I don't understand how my mother could be so selfish to leave us alone with Joe so that she could go and do whatever she wanted. Although my mom was irresponsible, to say the least, I'm grateful that in the end she was protective. She took us home immediately and I wonder if, despite her demons, she has some motherly instinct after all.

Fairytales

Two years later the hot dessert wind picks up the reddish sand and whips it around my face. I grab onto Dad's leg and steady myself until the wind dies down. I look up the road and see the sign that says, "Calico Ghost Town- Entrance". Today is our first family vacation and Dad let me pick where we get to go.

I learned about Calico Ghost town from my sister who learned about it in school. I bet it looks just like the old TV show *Wild Wild West* that Dad bought at a thrift store for me. He thought it was a cool idea to come see a real Wild West town, so he took a whole day off of work and drove us down here. I even get to miss a whole day of first grade so we can explore the town.

Calico Ghost Town sits in the mountains of the Mojave Desert near Barstow in San Bernardino, just two hours away from home. The calico colored hills gave the town its name after silver was found and the small town popped up. The town held, at one point: three hotels, five general stores, three restaurants, a school, post office, sheriff station, a few doctors, bars and brothels, and even a meat market. Calico was California's largest silver producer in the 1800's and had over five hundred mines with a population of 1200 until they found the mineral borate. Once the mineral was found the population reached

3500 and had many internationals from China, England, Ireland, Greece, France, and the Netherlands.

After 1896, the value of the silver went down because of the Silver Purchase Act which made the little town dry up. By 1907 it was completely abandoned. After several years it was purchased by Walter Knott, owner of Knott's Berry Farm, and he decided to restore the town based off of old photos. A few of the old buildings are left standing, and those are the ones I want to see the most.

"Hold my hand, Teester. The wind is kind of strong right now and I don't want you to blow away into a cactus or accidentally find a tribe of Indians!" Dad holds my hand tight and smiles. I like when he smiles. He has been smiling a lot lately and I think it's because Mom has a new baby in her tummy. I know it's a boy. After we got to move back home Mom and Dad have been happy. They don't fight as much.

"Heinrich, can you carry my backpack?" Mom asks. Her face is bright red already and I know she probably doesn't feel too good. She hates being hot. Dad made us come to Calico in the spring, hoping for cool weather, but it's already around 90 degrees and it's still morning.

"Sure. Why don't you drink some water?" He pulls out a water bottle before putting the backpack on. Mom takes a few drinks and then hands it to Emma. Emma drinks the rest and throws it on the ground.

"Litter-er! The Ghosts are going to haunt you, stupid!" I say. I pick up the water bottle.

"You're so dumb. There are no such things as ghosts." Emma is breathing heavy and I wonder if it's because she's getting fat. Deep down I feel a little satisfaction that she is gaining so much weight. She is already 140 pounds and is only 11 years old. I like that after so many years of her teasing me, I can

57

now tease her back. Whenever I mention her weight she tries to pretend it doesn't bother her, but I can tell she's unhappy. Sometimes, after I have called her fat, I see her doing jumping jacks in her room. I look over at her. Her round face is red and sweaty. I start to feel bad for her until she kicks a rock at me.

"Ghost are real and I'm going to make them haunt you until you die," I say, running out of range and throwing the water bottle into a trash can.

"Girls, stop fighting. Today is supposed to be fun, alright?" Dad says. "Let's go exploring!"

After walking up the small hill to the entrance, Dad pays for us. The woman at the counter is wearing a bonnet and a funny old dress. She hands Dad a map and points to a few spots. Dad makes us walk over to a little wooden bench and we all sit down.

"Let's plan out what we want to do, that way we have enough time to do all the fun stuff," he says pointing at the map. "I think we should pan for gold, explore the museum, see the reenactment show and go down into the mines." He points to each thing and I can't decide what sounds more fun.

"Can we see the old buildings too. The ones that were really here when the cowboys were?" I ask.

"There were no cowboys. Just miners," Emma says in a bossy voice, rolling her eyes.

"I meant miners." I smile at her. Despite out fighting, I like having her around. Sometimes she can even be fun.

"There are a few original buildings left that we could go visit," Dad says.

"That's boring. I want to go to the market and pick out some snacks," Emma whines.

"Then maybe Mom can take you to the market and I'll take Tara around to the old boring stuff and we will meet back here in an hour?" Dad looks at Mom and she nods.

"Come on, Dad. Let's go find the saloon!" I pull his hand but before he gets up he kisses Mom.

"Eww, that's gross. Let's go see the fun stuff, you can kiss mom later!" I say.

Dad laughs and lets me pull him down the old dusty street. There is a little wooden fence that goes around the walkway and little gates to let you explore what's behind it. The buildings all look old and wooden, but I know some of them are fake. I look up the road and see a really old building.

It's made of the same red colored dirt as the hills behind it. Some of the walls are even crumbling in places. I guess they used the dirt to make the walls. There is a little wooden boardwalk in front of the door, with a small wooden fence surrounding it. Above the board walk is a wooden covering to probably keep the sun off of you if you sit in the old rocking chain on the boardwalk. There are a few big windows in the front of the building next to the big wooden door.

I run up to it and walk onto the boardwalk. The old rocking chair moves a little in the wind and I wonder if there is a ghost sitting it in.

"Dad, it's a ghost!"

"I bet it's Lucy," he says.

"Who's Lucy?" I ask watching the rocking chair sway.

"She lived here. She was raised in Calico during the silver rush and then ran the store with her husband. She lived here until she died when she was 93 years old." Dad reads from a sign in the window. "This was her house and now is the museum. It's one of the original buildings in Calico and is said to be haunted by Lucy."

My eyes get big and I watch the rocking chair. It doesn't move anymore, but I'm sure it was Lucy. "Can we go inside?"

"Sure."

He pulls open the wooden door and we walk inside. The floor is a light golden wood and the light streams in from the windows. There are glass cases that looks like bookcases all along the red walls. They are filled with old pictures of the town and small nuggets of silver. There's some miners gloves and hats in the case and I wonder how it was mining for silver. I guess they just dug around until they found it.

Dad explains things to me as we make our way around the museum. The back door opens and I know I'm going to see Lucy, but an old man in funny clothes comes in and smiles.

"Welcome, Folks. How're you guys doing?" he says, with a scratchy voice. His white hair puffs out behind his ears making him look funny.

"Just fine," Dad smiles.

"Can I help you with anything?"

Dad looks at me before saying, "Could you tell us about Lucy's ghost?"

His face cracks into a million different lines when he smiles. His skin reminds me of old tree bark. "Well, Lucy was a great woman and lived here most of her life. When she died she was buried on the hill in the cemetery and every now and then," he pauses and winks at me, "If someone believes in her she will come visit."

"Really?" I whisper.

"Yes, she is often seen walking around the street or sitting in her rocking chair on nice days like today."

I look at Dad. His eyes are wide and he looks surprised. "See Tara, we must have seen her out on the walkway today!" His voice is loud and excited.

"Well, if you see her again, don't be afraid. She is a sweet ghost." The old man smiles and hands me a piece of candy.

"Thanks," Dad says for me and opens the door.

I open my salt water taffy and suck on it while watching the rocking chair for any signs of Lucy. I look out over the town and wonder how many ghosts live here. There had been so many people here at one point, it's weird that it is now so empty.

"Come on Tara, we've got to go meet Mom and Emma and then we will go panning for gold."

I look at the rocking chair one last time and can almost see an old woman sitting in it. I wave goodbye and follow dad down the dusty road. Mom and Emma are sitting on the bench eating an ice cream cone.

"I saw a ghost!" I announce and grab the cone mom hands me.

"That's great, Tara. Was is scary?" Mom asks.

"Nope, she's a nice ghost."

"How're you guys?" Dad asks.

"It's so hot. I hate it here," Emma grumbles.

"Well we can go pan for gold up the hill. You get to play in cold water for a while and if you find any gold you get to keep it." Dad points up to the top of the hill where there is a stream and a wooden hut next to it.

"Let's go!" I run up the hill past old wagons and stinky donkeys. I bet I will find some gold and then I can buy something cool with it. Maybe we can go to the gift shop. I run so fast that I'm the first one there. I wait in line and by the time Emma makes it to me it's our turn.

The worker hands us each a little pan and shows us how to get some of the dirt in the bottom of the stream and swish it around with the water. I swish too hard and all the dirt goes flying.

"Try a little softer, Teester," Mom says. She is leaning against the wooden fence and holding her belly. It's pretty big and I wonder how big my little brother is going to get before he comes out. I hope he keeps Mom and Dad happy like this.

"I found a piece!" I scream and pull out the nugget. It shines in the light and I wonder how rich I am now. The worker puts it in a little bag for me and I keep searching for more gold until I'm soaking wet.

"Let's go dry off a little," Dad says.

"Can we go to the gift store?"

"Sure," he says.

"We're going to stay here until you come back." Mom's face is bright red again and she looks sick.

"I'll be back in a minute and then we can go down in the mines. It's cold down there and will make you feel better." Dad rubs her belly before kissing her cheek. She smiles weakly and waves at me.

"Dad, come on!" I say, pulling his arm down towards town. We find the gift shop and open the door. I look around and see so many cool toys. I want to get something with my gold that says Calico on it.

"What can I help you with?" A woman in a long sleeve dress asks form behind the counter. She has a bonnet on and a white apron too. She must be so hot.

"How much can I get with this?" I hand her my gold nugget.

She looks at Dad and he laughs. "Tara, she has to weigh your gold to know how much it's worth, why don't you look around for a minute." He points to the stuffed animal section and I see a little coyote. I run to him and pick him up. He has a blue bandanna on his back that says Calico and fits right into my hand.

I turn around just in time to see dad pass the girl some money. I wonder what he is buying. I run back to the woman and hand her my coyote.

"Will the gold be enough for him?" I worry that it won't be and that Dad doesn't have any money either. I hope I can get him.

She puts him on top of the cash register and presses a button. "You choose the perfect thing!" she says, "Your gold even covers a few more dollars' worth of something if you want." She looks at Dad.

"Can you add some of the salt water taffy until it's all used?" Dad asks.

"Sure." She puts my coyote into a plastic bag and tosses a few hand fulls of candy into it as well.

"Thank you so much!" I say when she hands it to me.

"You did all the work finding that gold. Good job!" She waves goodbye.

"Dad, can I go get some more gold?" I ask. I think about all the other cool toys and the chocolate I saw sitting on the counter. If I find enough gold maybe I can get some of it.

"No, we promised to go down into the mines, remember?"

I shrug and say, "Ok." I find Mom and Emma sharing a water bottle on a bench near the store.

"Look at what my gold bought!" I hand her my bag and she dumps it out.

"He's so cute." Mom hands me the coyote and I give him a hug.

"It's fake gold, dummy," Emma says.

"Then how did I get all this stuff?"

"Dad probably just bought it for you." She throws a piece of candy into my face. It bounces off my nose before rolling away in the dust.

"Did not!" I push her shoulder so she falls off the bench.

Her round face is shocked when she lands in a heap at my feet. "Ugh, you're so dumb!" She swings at me but misses.

"You're too slow!" I taunt. I hope she chases me to the mines. That would be fun. I know that if I'm a brat to her she will. "You must be getting too fat to catch me!"

She glares at me and runs towards me. I laugh and run away. The mine entrance is at the top of a hill so I have to keep taunting Emma so she chases me. It's almost like we are playing tag. Except I can't really tell if she's playing or just really wants to hit me. Maybe it's both.

I reach the top of the hill first and sit in the shade. Emma is breathing so hard when she finally gets to me that I worry she is having an asthma attack. She collapses next to me and moans.

"You alright?" I ask.

"I hate this place," she wheezes.

"Girls, you ready to enter the mines?" Dad pulls Mom along behind him.

I jump up and open the door. The building is cold and it feels wonderful.

"How is it so cold in here?" I ask Dad.

"The mines go deep underground and the cold air travels up here," a man standing behind the counter says.

"So, a mine is like a cave?" I think about the goosebumps book I just finished. It was all about creepy cave creatures.

"Kind of," Dad says.

"I don't know if we should go in there." I hesitate for the first time today.

Dad knelt next to me and smiles. "Some caves are great. You know caves are known for being meeting places for lovers?" He wiggles his bushy white eyebrows up and down.

"Really?"

"Yes, sometimes the lovers had families that did not support the relationship. Sometimes they were even at war with each other. So, lovers would sneak off to the cave to meet in secret and be together."

"Is that how you met Mom?" I ask.

"No, but I can tell you about how we met as we walk through the mine." He opens the door leading to the beginning of the mine and holds out his hand to me. I take it and follow him inside.

The mine is dark and cold. The stone walls and floor make our footsteps echo. It looks like a tunnel going steadily down into the earth. How deep does it go? I wonder if there is anything hiding down there. I hug dads side and inch forward, slowly.

"You're such a baby," Emma says, pushing past me.

"I promised you a story, right?" Dad asks.

I smile and keep close to him as we walk further down into the darkness.

"Well, about ten years ago I was going through a rough patch. I was about to start law school but the woman I was married to divorced me out of the blue. I was depressed and couldn't stay in California. I decided to go live with my little sister in Nebraska for a while."

"That's where mom's from." I smile. We pass by a tiny light embedded into the stone. They have them every few hundred feet to help guide us through. But whenever I see them all I think about is what would happen if they stopped working. I shudder and squeeze dad's fingers.

"That's right. So when I get to Nebraska I got a job at the slaughter house but it was disgusting and I was miserable. I left that job and got a job at the factory. It wasn't as bad as the slaughter house but I was still pretty miserable. My sister set me up on a bunch of double dates to try to make me happy."

"So you dated Mom?"

"Not exactly." He smiles and looks at Mom. She smiles back and her nose kind of scrunches up a little bit. I think it's cute.

The mine begins to twist and turn. On either side of the walkway are huge caverns that are blocked off with chicken wire. There is just enough light to see how deep they go. Just when I start to panic, Dad grabs my hand again.

"I went on a blind date with some weirdo. We were supposed to meet up with another couple. I was sitting at our table in the diner when your mom walked in." He looks over at her and his voice gets quiet. "She was the most beautiful woman I had ever seen. Lots of curly hair, great body and beautiful green eyes."

Mom laughs and turns to me.

"Your dad ignored his date the entire time." A pleased smile fills her face.

"I couldn't focus on her when your foot was going up and down my leg."

"You were a sexy Californian, what was I supposed to do?" Moms cheeks turn a light pink.

Dad pulls mom in close and gives her a kiss on the cheek. She smiles and leans into him. She whispers into his ear and he laughs sending echoes down the mine. I like seeing them like this. It makes me happy. A crunching sound from down in the cave makes me look away from them. I turn to look down the path and notice that Emma is out of sight.

I speed up a little to look for her. Hopefully she didn't try to lean on the chicken wire walls leading into the caverns. With her weight I'm sure she would fall through. Just as I walk around the corner, she jumps out at me. I scream, but it's cut off when she punches me in the stomach. I drop to the ground, pain radiating though my body.

I glare up at her, "What'd you do that for?"

"You deserve it for calling me fat."

Mom comes into view holding Dad's hand onto her belly. "What's going on?" Her voice instantly fills with irritation.

"Nothing. Can we just get out of here now?" Emma asks.

"Yeah, let's go. I want to get drink." Mom catches up with Emma and they leave me behind.

Dad pulls my ponytail for a second before holding out his hand. I take it and pull myself up. I dust my knees off. I vow to get vengeance on her at some point.

"So, you and Mom moved to California after your date?" I ask, trying to hide my embarrassment for getting beaten up. Hopefully if I force Dad to talk about his story he won't ask about what happened with Emma.

"Well we went home together that night. We spent every possible moment together. But after a while I needed to come back to California. I had to finish my divorce and move on with my life. So, one day I packed up my truck and drove over to your grandma's house to say goodbye to your mom. When I got there, she threw a few bags into the bed of my truck, buckled Emma into the back, and climbed into the front seat. We didn't ever talk about it, we just drove to California."

At the time, I didn't appreciate the magic of their love story. I didn't think about how intense it must have been or how it helped my dad get through his divorce. All I knew was that they finally seemed happy now, like they were in the story. As we leave the mines and met up with Mom and Emma I'm happy. Happier than I have ever been. I never suspect that this fairytale moment won't last.

17 Weeks

Baby R Us is huge and a little overwhelming. The white floors gleam and match the toothy smiles from the toddlers on the boxes and signs I walk past. Bright pinks and purples signal the little girl section and the deep blues and greens mark the boys and I avoid it all. Quickly.

I don't want to look for clothing just yet. Seeing an outfit and knowing that eventually I will have two babies to dress makes my heart pound, so instead I walk to the back of the store. I wander around looking at cribs and rocking chairs until my feet hurt, so I sink into a dark brown rocking chair. I pull my water bottle from my bag and drink the entire thing. Closing my eyes, I slowly rock back and forth.

The twins begin to move and it startles me. I'm still not used to being able to feel them yet. This time instead of big movements, they are small and gentle. It feels almost like I have little bubbles moving around in my stomach. The little jabs and kicks in between the slow rolls feel more like my stomach is growling than anything at this point. Knowing that they are moving around and still growing make me feel like I am doing a good job so far. At least I know they are safe and happy.

"That looks comfy."

I open my eyes and see Alex standing over me. His hair is longer than normal and falls into his face as he leans down and gives me a kiss. He smiles before sinking into the rocking chair next to me. Putting his feet up on the little ottoman he sighs.

"You've got to put your feet up," he says. His voice is low and quiet. I can tell he is relaxed.

I laugh at him, but put my feet up anyway. The soft cushion cradles my sore feet and it even rocks back and forth with me.

"Aren't you happy you listened to me?" he asks.

"Yeah, we have got to get one of the chairs." I sink into the cushions and close my eyes again. I could fall asleep here and be completely happy. I almost do, but Alex stands up and grabs my hand.

"They're a bit pricey." He pulls me to my feet and we walk through all the different chairs. "Let's keep looking around for other things we might need."

"Let's go find the car seats before we decide on anything," I say.

"They're down here, I found them earlier when I was looking for the cribs."

Alex leads me down three different aisles before we find the car seat selection. They fill an entire wall all by themselves. I pull out a sheet of paper from my pocket and hand it to him.

"I'm feeling kind of sick, I'm going to sit down for a second. But these car seats are the top rated ones online. They are the best in accidents and child safety tests for this year and some of them are even convertible car seats so they fit the infant, then the toddler and then they convert to a booster seat for the young kid until they're big enough to not need one."

He looks at the list and nods before walking towards all the choices. I sit down on a few boxes that have been left in the aisle.

My heart beat starts to slow again and my breathing returns to normal. I hate how I can't even walk around a store anymore without feeling like I'm going to pass out, but I remind myself to take it easy. Growing two babies at once is not easy.

"I found the top three on your list. Want to come see?" Alex walks back towards me and holds out his hand. Even though I'm only 17 weeks and not very big yet, I still need help standing back up after sitting down. I can do it on my own, but when I do it puts a lot of pressure on my bladder and I feel like I'm about to pee my pants. I really want to avoid that, so Alex helps me whenever he can. I can only imagine how it will be when my belly is bigger.

Alex leads me down the row and stops in front of a display of car seats. They are so big I wonder if it really will be safe for an infant. The first one Alex points at looks like it would fill the entire area in the backseat meant for one person. The back is high and has a bunch of clasps and buckles attached to it. There is a removable cushion for the infant, and then a larger one for the toddler. There is even a little cup hold on one side and arm rest on the other. It's black with a little grey stars and moons on it but can come in a variety of colors.

"This one is the top rated one. Best on accidents from all different angles and for comfort and stuff. It has the price tag to go along with it, too."

I read the entre label and feel the little infant insert that is supposed to help hold the baby's head in place. It's soft and seems like it would be comfortable.

"How much is this one?" I ask, dreading the answer.

"Three hundred and eighty."

I nod, slowly, and look at the next one in line. This one is still just as big, but there is no arm rest, no cup holder and its plain black, but the label claims that it is just as safe as the last one.

"What about this one?" I ask.

"It's three hundred and twenty. Babe, I want the twins to be safe but we can't afford to buy two of these things and all the rest of the stuff we need for them."

"Maybe not these ones, but we have to get a top rated one and getting a convertible will save us money in the long run. We will only have to buy one car seat instead of upgrading car seats each time the girls hit a certain weight. I want them to be safe. I know what it's like to need a car seat and not be in one." I remember the trees zipping by the window and how I had flown up and hit the roof while going over a bump with mom all those years ago. "I'll give up my rocker so we can get a little more expensive car seat for them, alright?"

"But won't you want the chair to nurse in and sleep in with them?"

"It would have been nice, but I'd rather have them have everything they need and make sure they have a really safe car seat before I get myself a chair."

"Alright, well let's go down the list a little. There are some that are still rated pretty safe but are closer to one hundred dollars down here."

After browsing for almost an hour, we settle on a few convertible car seats that are a little over one hundred dollars each. They are plain, but the reviews and test all rate them as being safe.

"You want to rock for a few minutes before we leave?" Alex asks.

"Yeah, I want to say goodbye to it." I laugh.

We both sit down into the most expensive rocking chairs they have on display and sit for a few minutes before picking up our car seats and leaving.

Time to Party

I pat my leg and the kitten runs to me. "You can't tell Mom or Emma where my spot is. It's a secret." Tabby Sue just rubs on my legs and purrs. I found the hiding place just before I started first grade. It has been almost a year now and I still love my hiding place. I like having a spot that I can go to play. It's a little cubby behind a bunch of trees. The branches bend down and make a little ceiling and you have to be skinny to get in, so I know I'm the only one who will get in. I still don't want Mom or Emma to find it, so I always sneak there. Tabby meows and rubs on my hand.

"Now you start on the top stair. Then you count to seven. That's how many jumps you have to do." I jump down the wide stairs seven times.

"Then you have to spin around once." I spin. I grab Tabby's tail and make him spin too.

"Ok Sue, you've made it so far. Now you have to run to the end of the kennel, ready?"

I look past the kennel that our three dogs live in and into the meadow next to our house. It's just empty until you get to the back. That's where all the trees are and my secret place too. Wiggling my toes I wait for Tabby Sue. He stares at my toes then crouches down. He is about to pounce. I run. He chases me past the kennel and into the yard.

I jump over some gopher holes and Tabby Sue follows my every move. Once I hit the dirt patch near the back I stop and Tabby runs into my legs.

"Now you have to be careful, Sue. There are Indians and cowboys all over these parts," I whisper. "Let's hurry and get into my secret clubhouse before they catch us in a Wild West battle." I tiptoe into the thicket of pine trees and go to the very back of the lot. I circle around a clump of skinny tall trees and find the opening. It's a little hole that is partially covered by a bush. I move the branches out of the way and squeeze inside. The trees grow in an oval shape. They must have started out with a lot of space between them, but as they got thicker they got closer together making them all almost touch forming a nearly solid wall of tree. The center was empty and I made it my little secret room.

"Come on Sue, it's like our own little teepee." Mom always says that her family has Native American blood in there somewhere and I like to pretend it is true while in my teepee. I can hear Tabby Sue outside, but he doesn't come in. I poke my head out. He is sitting right in front of the hole and rolls onto his back when he sees me.

"It's not time for a dirt bath! There could be an attack by savages at any time!" I pull him inside before any cowboys can get him.

Inside it's just big enough for me to sit cross legged with a little pathway for him to walk around. He sniffs the inside of the teepee and scratched one of the trees it's made of.

"See Sue, I've got lots of cool stuff in here." I show him where I keep the rocks I find all lined up on the bottom of each tree and where I hang some of the bird feathers I find up in the branches. I have a little stash of snacks, too, but they have to sit just outside my secret spot, hidden in the bush that helps cover the door. I grab a little box that has some raisins in it and let Tabby sniff them.

He tries to eat one, so I lay it out on the floor and shove a few in my mouth. I love raisins. They're so good, almost like candy. I like how they are all wrinkled and stick together too, because that way you always get a bunch with each bite. I used to bring them to school until everyone started calling me 'The Raisin'. I didn't like it. So now I just eat them when I come into my hiding place.

"This is the best place ever, Tabby Sue. I wish we could live out here, but it's too small." He nudges my hand, so I give him another raisin. He bites into it and chokes a little before swallowing it. I reach outside the door and grab a water bottle. I pour the water into the lid and let him lick it out.

"I wish we could stay in here until the party is over. I hate parties," I tell Tabby. I can hear music drift over form my house and hope that no one will notice that I'm gone. Mom likes to throw parties when Dad works the night shift as a security guard down at the juvenile hall. He's gone all night so Mom has friends over until early in the morning. Today Dad left early, right after dinner at six, so Mom started early.

She called all the neighbors and went to the store for beer. She got a few boxes of it. I hate when she drinks it. She acts weird. So, most of the time I play with Tabby Sue or read.

I stand up and reach as high as I can in my teepee until I feel the Ziploc bag. I pull it down and open it. I hide books out here so that I have something to read when I hide.

"Come inside and talk with real people." Mom yells from the deck. Her voice is too loud and her words all slur together. My heart sinks. I know she will force me to come inside eventually, but I act like I don't hear her. Maybe I will get a few minutes more to myself.

"She just talks with the cat and reads those damn books. She's not a normal seven-year-old." Her voice carries through the loud music and over the meadow. Isabel, our neighbor, laughs.

"It's not my fault I only like you, Tabby. You're the only one who's nice." I pull him into my lap and bury my face in his fur. He smells like dirt, but I don't mind. He starts to knead my hair and purr. He's so loud that it vibrates my chest. I scratch him behind the ears for a few minutes before climbing out of my secret spot. Tabby tries to follow me, but I push him back inside.

"I don't want them to cut your whiskers off again, Sue. Stay here until I come get you." He meows a few times but then rolls up into a ball and goes to sleep. I walk towards the house. Dreading every step.

"Come on T, we're playing tag!" My brother Finn screams as he runs around the living room, only wearing his shorts. I smile at his nickname for me. I guess little brothers always give nicknames because they can't pronounce names the right way when they are so little. I like when he calls me 'T'. I stand in the doorway and watch as Amanda and Sammy, the neighbor's kids, chase him, laughing. Sammy's hair is black and so curly that it sticks up around her face. It barely moves as she runs around the small coffee table. I watch Mom and Isabel get more beer out of the fridge. They're talking loudly to hear each other over the music, and they tease Emma while she stirs the boiling pot on the stove. Emma smiles and shoves of piece of her red hair behind her ear.

The steam from the pot fills the kitchen with heat. I instantly get a head ache from it and the music. It's so loud that I can't hear what they're singing about. I sneak through the kitchen and weave through the other kids running around until I make it to the couch.

I jump into the large pile of blankets on the end of the couch and prop my newest *Nancy Drew* up against my knees after digging it out of the cushions. I went to the library yesterday with Dad and Finn and I got to pick out anything I wanted. I love Nancy Drew; she always knows what to do to save the day. I read a few pages before I can't focus anymore. Finn keeps bumping my knees when he runs by me and Isabel and Mom are sitting at the kitchen table, opening new beers. Their whisper's somehow float over the music. I always feel like they're talking about me. I hate it. I hear little comments about my hair and my clothes from them. The familiar feeling of warmth spreads into my ears and face. I know now that there was no reason for me to feel so embarrassed but sitting on the couch I feel like I am under a spotlight. I feel like I don't belong.

After a while I sneak into the bathroom. It's tiny and cold but somehow quiet. It's the only room in the house with a lock, so I know I can be alone for a while. I sit on the closed toilet and read a few chapters before Mom pounds on the door.

"Get out here now!" Her voice is slurred, and I know that if I try to stay I will get into big trouble.

She rips my book out of my hands when I open the door. "Eat your dinner and play with your friends." She stumbles to the fridge and puts my book on top of it, where she knows I can't reach it. Her sweatpants and baggy shirt hang off her. This is her favorite outfit for when she is too fat for her skinny clothes but starting to lose weight because of the drugs she likes to do.

Isabel laughs and opens another beer. Her face is red. "Books won't do you any good Tara."

I ignore her and take a bowl of hamburger helper into the living room and sit on the floor with Finn. Amanda and Finn are eating out of the same bowl. Her hair is long and straight and tickles Finn's arm. He pushes it out of the way before taking another bite.

"What were you doing in there for so long?" Sammy smiles. Her hair puffs out around her face and reminds me of clouds.

"I was reading." I take a big bite and chew slow so that I don't have to talk anymore. No one else likes reading except Dad. They all think it's weird.

"Stop trying to pretend you're smart, Tara. It's not working." Emma laughs and takes her bowl into the kitchen for seconds. I wonder if she is right, just for a second. But then I push the thought away. I know I'm smart. And if not, I'll work extra hard to learn more. I'll do anything I can to not be like her or Mom.

"Want to play Legos with me, T?" Finn drops his food on the floor and crawls over to the toy bucket to grab the bag of Legos.

"Ok, let's see who can build the tallest tower" I say.

We all start to build towers. Finn's falls over first since he is only two years old and can't build very well. I laugh. I hand him some of my Legos and help him to start another tower. We keep building until all of us run out of Legos.

"Hey Finn, you wanna be a monster and knock them over?" I point to the little city of towers and buildings we made. Finn's eyes get big and he kicks them all over the room.

"Are you kidding me?" Mom walks into the room. Finn freezes and looks like he is about to cry. Mom rubs his hair before turning to me.

"Tara, *you* get to pick up the mess now." Mom collapses onto the couch with Isabel. I'm glad I moved my book, or she would have squished it. I start to pick up the Legos as Finn runs around kicking things and growling.

"Finn come here and stop kicking shit around." Mom picks him up and puts him next to her. "You want some beer?"

"Is it yummy?" Finn holds out his hands.

"Yeah, it's real good." Mom laughs and hands him her can. He takes a small drink and makes a face. I dump the last of the Legos back into the toy box and turn to look at Finn. He's too little to be drinking beer. I don't know why Mom would even give it to him. Even at seven years old I know that beer is not something a toddler should be drinking. I worry that he will get sick. I also worry that he will start to be mean to me, too.

"Try it again little man, it gets better." Isabel pushes the can back into his mouth.

He takes a few more drinks and smiles. "Can I have it?"

"You can have it if you don't spill, now go play." Mom pulls a new can from the box near her feet and watches TV with Isabel.

Finn sits next to me and takes a drink. The bubbles from inside the can make me want to sneeze. He just laughs. I pull the beer away from him and walk into the kitchen. I know I will get in trouble, but I don't care; I'm not letting him keep it. Finn cries and follows me, pulling my shirt and trying to take the beer back.

"Give me my beer!" His voice is loud and whinny.

"No."

"It's mine!"

"Well, it's not now." I pour it down the sink. Dad told me that beer isn't good for you. Finn shouldn't be drinking half a can all by himself. He probably shouldn't have any of it at all. I think about how Mom acts when she has been drinking beer. She likes to hit me and doesn't mind kicking or cutting the whiskers off the cat. She yells, stumbles around, and forgets to change Finn's diaper or even feed him. I don't want Finn to be like that.

"Mom, Tara took my beer!" Finn runs into the living room, crying, and pulls at Mom.

She glares at me from her seat. I watch as she walks into the kitchen, stumbles, and holds onto the counter. Leaning down, she pulls the neck of my shirt up until I'm in her face. My feet hang a little above the floor. Her breath is warm and stinky. "I gave that to him, what makes you think *you* can take it away?"

"It's not good for him. He's only two."

"Are *you* the mom?"

"Dad said beer's not good…"

"I don't give a fuck what your dad said. You don't get to tell Finn what he can and can't have. Now go away." She shoves me until I almost fall over.

My heart pounds and I feel the angry tears filling my eyes. I hate when I get in trouble for taking care of Finn. Mom should be happy that I help with him when she's busy with her friends. The responsibility of taking care of a two-year-old should never have been placed on my shoulders. Especially due to drug and alcohol abuse. A seven-year-old should be worried about playing with toys and watching cartoons, not the life and welfare of a toddler.

I stand up and tap moms shoulder. She turns back to me with her hand raised. I flinch before I realize that she was reaching for a can of beer that's on the counter.

"Can I have my book back?"

She gets my book from the top of the fridge and throws it into the living room. It lands under our square dinner table. I crawl under it and grab my book. I don't know why mom wants me to stay downstairs, but I know that if I try to go upstairs she will throw a fit, so I stay under the table. Tabby Sue runs into the house and jumps in my lap. I open the book and start to read while holding him tight. I don't want anything to happen to him. He's my only friend.

"What a prude! Tara you're such a good little girl." Isabel yells at me from the couch. She gets up and walks over to the table. She sticks her face under it and grins at me. Mom walks in and looks at me too. My ears get red and I can feel my heart beat in them.

"Look at her. Such an ugly, fat little girl. Daddy's little *princess* with her books and her cat. She thinks she's better than everyone, but I know better. She's just a stupid girl who doesn't have any friends." Mom laughs and points at my book. "Only those damn books like her."

I turn the page without seeing the words. I blame their behavior on the alcohol. But thinking about it now while writing this I wonder if it was something more. I wonder if I was just too different. Maybe I was just too much like my dad. Or maybe Mom knew that somehow, I had more potential than she did, even at seven years old.

After a night of partying Mom is taking a shower. She didn't even sleep but now she wants to go to a friend's house and told me to get Finn ready. I don't want to go. Maybe if Finn isn't ready and Mom is still feeling sick we can just stay home. She threw up a lot last night and I hope she has the flu.

"Tara, what are you supposed to be doing right now?" Mom runs upstairs to get dressed. She is still dripping from her shower. I know that if I don't get Finn ready right now I will get a spank. I wish I could stay home like Emma can, but I guess I'm not old enough. It's my job to watch Finn. I get up and open the small closet in between the kitchen and the living room. It's full of shoes and coats and with no light I have to dig around for his snow boots. They're the only ones I can put on him because I don't have to tie the laces. I'm still not very good at tying the laces. Sometimes they stay tied but a lot of the time they just come loose.

"Finn, give me your feet." I crawl onto the army sleeping bag and hit the blanket looking for his feet.

"No, T." Finn starts to squirm away from me.

"We have to get your shoes on." I try to pin him down but he's fast. He crawls away and starts to laugh. "Finn, come on. Mom's gonna be downstairs in a few minutes and she'll be mad if your shoes aren't on." I swing his boots in front of him. Mom wouldn't be mad at Finn, she'd be mad at me. If this doesn't work I'll try to find a piece of candy.

"You do it." Finn sticks his feet out to me and wiggles his toes. I put his socks on and slip his feet inside his boots. He tries to crawl back into bed but I grab him.

"Do you have to go potty?" He's been learning to use the real bathroom, so I have to ask him every time before we leave the house.

"No." He smiles. I know he has to go.

"Go to the bathroom and you get a piece of candy."

He sits still for a second thinking about the candy. Then he gets up and runs to the bathroom. Hopefully he doesn't pee on the floor again. I walk to the big bookcase Dad built last summer. It was fun. I got to help him hold the wood together while he put the nails in. I like to hide my candy in the bookcase. It's always behind the old, pretty books. The ones Dad finds at thrift stores. I always like to open them because they smell really good, but I can't read most of the words. They're too big for me.

Behind my favorite book there's a jolly rancher. It's a purple one, so I don't care if Finn gets it. I don't really like the purple ones. I put the book back just as he runs out of the bathroom. He's smiling so he must have gone.

"Did you flush and wash your hands?" I dangle the candy in front of him.

"Mm-hmm. Give me the candy."

"If you get your coat on."

Finn slips on his jacket and holds his hand out for the candy. I give it to him and sit on the couch waiting for Mom to come downstairs.

Once she's ready, we pile into the car and drive up the road. Allison lives up the big hill and around the corner from us. We go to her house a lot. Mom parks in the drive way and goes inside before I can even unbuckle myself. I unbuckle Finn and pull him out. The stones in front of the door are broken and I have to hold Finn, so he doesn't fall over.

"Remember not to touch Elvis." Elvis is one of Allison's dogs. Allison has a lot of dogs, but Elvis is the one to watch. He is old, mean, stinky, and he likes to sneak up on you. Finn likes Elvis though. He's always trying to pet him.

I knock on the big wooden door. It's too heavy for me to open and the rule is I have to knock before someone lets me in.

"Hold on Tara." Mom yells. There are people laughing inside. After a minute Mom opens the door a crack. We can never open the door all the way or the dogs will get out. After I shove Finn inside, I squeeze through.

The living room is dark because the blinds are always closed and the only lamp is always off. The floor is concrete and cold so I never take my shoes off. Finn runs to the couch and jumps onto it, making a cloud of dog hair fly into the room. I watch it flutter down and land on the ground before following him. I hate how much dog hair there always is. I sit down slowly, trying to keep the hair from floating around again. The old TV is sitting on a crate in front of the couch and if I get lucky and move the metal thing on top just right, the picture will be normal, and we can hear the words. If not, we just have to make the voices ourselves. I hate doing that because I never know what the people are supposed to say and if I take too long Finn with get mad.

"Terrible Tara, come here." Allison says from the kitchen. I push past the dirty sheet that's hanging up where the door should be to get to her. I think the sheet used to be white but now it's yellow and brown. The kitchen isn't any better. The floor hasn't been cleaned in a long time and it makes my shoes sound like plunger-feet like in the cartoons. I like being in the kitchen better though because it has two big windows that don't have curtains. It's always sunnier in here.

"Give me a hug, Terrible. I'm sorry I missed your party. I can't believe you're seven now." Allison opens her arms. She's standing by the windows and her yellow hair glows in the light. I give her a hug and she holds me tight. She likes hugs. "Can you do me a big favor today since you're so grown up?"

"You want me to let the dogs outside, right?" I always watch the dogs when we come over because Mom and Allison are too busy upstairs. I think it's because I'm good at doing chores, but looking back on it, I know it was because they were too busy doing drugs and drinking to do anything else.

"Yes, and I need you to feed them later too. Their food is in the closet, just throw some in the yard and let them eat out there ok?" She pats my head and grabs a bag of groceries.

"Natalie, come on!" She calls over to Mom and they both go upstairs together. I have never been upstairs before.

After watching TV for a while the dogs need to be let out. I take Finn with me into the kitchen and open the door and all six of the dogs run past, excited to finally be outside. The back yard is small and smelly, but Finn likes to play with the dogs out there. I open the dog food, fill a big bowl and, when I walk outside, the dogs knock me over for the food. Allison doesn't do a good job feeding them and I know they're hungry. I scrape my knee and it bleeds a little, but I don't let Finn see because he gets scared.

"Come on Finn, I don't want them to eat us too!" I pull him inside and slam the door.

"T, I'm hungry." Finn pulls on my hand.

"I'll get something if you go watch TV or play in the living room."

He runs into the living room and I hear him pull the toys out of the toy box Allison keeps by the door. I look around the kitchen for food. There isn't anything in the cupboards or on the counter but empty bags. I open the fridge and find a bowl of soup that has dark green and black fuzz on top of it. I push it to the back of the fridge so I can't smell it. There's a squishy apple in the bottom of the fridge, but when I pick it up it falls apart. My stomach growls and I remember the bag of food Allison brought upstairs.

I'm not allowed upstairs, but I need to find food for Finn, so I go anyway. I'll do anything for him. The stairs are covered in carpet that smells like dog. They squeak as I walk up them and I feel like I'm going to fall through, but I make it to the top. There are a few doors that are open, but no one is inside the dark rooms. The door at the end of the hall is closed and the light is on, so I sneak to it. There are piles of clothes and boxes everywhere and I have to be careful not to bump anything. The hall starts to get stinky as I get close to the door, but I knock anyways, not realizing that the fumes seeping from under the door are from the drugs that are burning in the room. For a minute nothing happens and then Allison opens the door. I see a big plant behind her that has its own light.

"That's a cool plant. Are you growing it? You know, I garden with Dad sometimes and we grow lots of stuff."

Allison laughs and pulls me inside. "It's one of my favorite plants. Your mom likes it too. You want to see it?" The room is dark except for the light on the plant. Mom is lying in bed facing the other way.

"Why is there foil behind it?" The plant is in a pot on its own table. It has dark green leaves that are wide and pointy. Years later I will see these plants again during red ribbon week. A Sheriff will come to talk to us about marijuana and how smoking it is bad. But that will be years from now, and as a seven-year-old I just think the plant is pretty.

"Because it needs a lot of heat and the foil helps it stay warm."

"That's cool. It's almost as tall as Finn! You're a good gardener!"

Allison laughs and sits down on the bed. "I've had this plant a long time. It's good that it's almost as tall as a two-year-old. That means I get to enjoy it anytime I want."

"What do you want, Tara?" Mom glares at me from the bed.

"Finn's hungry and there's no food downstairs."

Mom sighs and rubs her face. "You know you're not allowed to be up here. Just go downstairs. We'll go home soon; you can eat then."

"Hold on, did you feed the dogs like I asked?" Allison pulls my face until it's close to hers. Her breath smells bad, but I don't say anything.

"Yes."

Allison smiles and reaches over the side of the bed. A bag rustles and she hands me ten crackers. "Is that good for you?"

"Tara! Get out! I came *up* here to get the hell away from you." Mom shoves me out of the door before I can thank

Allison for the crackers. Mom slams the door and I can hear them laughing. I run downstairs so I can't hear what they're saying. I find Graf playing on the floor with some trucks.

"I'm hungry." Finn's whinny voice is starting to come out. That means he's going to throw a fit soon. I show him the crackers and he holds out his hands. I hand him all of them and my stomach growls.

Santa's Village

Today is my third grade field trip and I am a little nervous because Mom agreed to be a chaperone. I hope she didn't do any drugs this morning. I stare out of my window and watch Santa's Village come into sight. Little cabins with snow filled windows rise above the parking lot. They are bright colors and there are a lot of people dressed as elves walking around. It looks a little silly, but I'm too excited to care much. Mom finds a place in the back of the lot and shuts the car off.

"You ready to meet Santa and see his workshop?" Mom smiles and pulls her jacket from the back of the Volkswagen. She slips her arms in and rubs then to warm up.

"Mom, I know Santa isn't real," I roll my eyes. My sister told me when I was three that he didn't really exist. "I just want to ride the bumper cars and the train and the zip line!" I jump out of the car and start walking towards the entrance.

"Tara, wait. You need to put on your jacket and your gloves, its freezing out here!" Mom chases after me and hands me my things.

"Fine, I'll put them on, but hurry! I want to see if there are any reindeer and elves and... Oh look!" I point to the entrance. The path is lined with candy canes that are taller than Mom. It snowed last night and the pathway is a little slippery, but it looks so pretty. I impatiently wait in line while Mom checks in with the ticket lady. She hands Mom a packet and points to the bright red gate.

"Come on, T, we have to fill out these papers as we go through the park. It's part of your homework, but as soon as that's done we can go on as many rides as you want." She smiles.

Mom look a lot happier since she has been getting better. I guess she was sick. But Dad made her go get a few tests done and after a few days in bed she was able to get up and has been doing a lot of things. She got a job at church and takes me with her sometimes so I can sit in the library. I didn't know at the time, but she had been detoxing and testing for sexually transmitted diseases after her latest drug filled weekend.

I look at her and notice that she is thin now and her eyes are large. They're a pretty green with brown specks in them that Mom says are like freckles. Her long curly hair is pulled up into a ponytail and she has on purple ear muffs. I hope I'm just as pretty when I'm older.

"Ok, but let's hurry!" I grab the papers and start the scavenger hunt.

After finding the last item on the list, drawing a picture of it and writing a sentence about it, I hand the paper back to Mom. She looks it over, shoves it in the envelope and gives me a high five.

"What do you want to go on first?" She asks, smiling.

I look around the village. It is as big as my entire school, filled with little cabins that are gift shops and cafes. They are all bright pink or green or blue and have little decorations hanging in all the windows. There is a huge decorated Christmas tree in the center with gifts underneath. There are lots of little painted mushrooms, and workers dressed up as elves run all over the place. Santa's house is right in the middle and I guess you can go and meet him, even though he is just pretending.

If there really was a workshop in the North Pole, it would look just like this I think. I watch other kids run towards the petting zoo filled with fuzzy animals and some parents get onto rides with their children. I don't know what to do first. It's all so fun. Christmas music plays over loud speakers and Mom grabs my hand. I can feel how warm it is through my mittens as she pulls me towards the back of the park.

"Where are we going?" I stomp through the snow and try to ignore how my feet are getting wet. I hate when my socks are wet but I guess it doesn't matter as long as I get to go on some rides.

"There is a train track over here and I think you get to drive little sleighs around. You want to go on it? I know how much you like to drive."

I nod eagerly and race ahead, pulling Mom after me. The line isn't too long, and before I know it I'm sitting in a little red train. The worker straps me in and Mom waves at me from the gate.

I grab the steering wheel as it takes off around the track. It cruises through snowbanks and past tiny model cabins. There are tiny elves working on toys and even a few snowmen who wave and dance. I try to turn the wheel, to follow the track, but my mittens slip. The sleigh follows the curve of the track anyways, but I want to be able to pretend that I'm driving. I pull my mittens off and yank the wheel. It turns and the sleigh seems to go even faster.

I whip around a bend and see Mom standing at the gate waving. As I zip past her she yells at me to put on my mittens, but I can't take my hands off of the wheel because I'm going so fast. I laugh for the rest of the ride and I don't stop even when the train slows down and the workers come around to unstrap me.

"Put your mittens back on," Mom says as I find her in the crowd.

"Can you help me?" I ask. My fingers are numb, and I can't open the clasps myself.

Mom takes my gloves from my hands. "You're freezing cold!" She rubs my hands in between hers and blows on them. Mom looks like a dragon each time she blows on my hands because her warm breath billows around my fingers like smoke. The warm air feels good on them. I shiver involuntarily. "Let's go inside and get something warm to eat." She points to the café behind me.

I hold onto her hand and we walk inside together. The café is warm and has a crackling fire in the fireplace along one wall. The menu hangs up above the cashier and mom orders two bowls of chili and two medium cokes. We sit close to the fire on little chairs shaped like mushrooms. The table is a bigger mushroom that is painted a neon green and purple.

The chili is perfect. "This is nice, Teester."

I smile over my bowl at mom who smiles back. We finish our chili quietly and drink our sodas together.

"You warm enough to head back out?" Mom asks.

I wiggle my toes and wish they were dry. "Can we stand by the fire for a minute first?" I ask.

"You go ahead, and I will be right back." She heads out the door.

I pull my gloves back on and stand next to the fire. I make sure my toes are pointed towards the warmth so that my socks will dry. I watch the orange and red flames dance together. I like how they always seem to be revolving around each other. Sometimes they look like they are fighting and other times they look like they are merging together.

"Close your eyes." Mom says, from behind me.

"Why?" I try to turn around, but mom wraps her arms around me. In her hands is a little package wrapped in tissue paper.

"What is that?" I reach for it and she lets it go. I rip the red and green tissue paper off and drop it on the floor. Whatever the gift is, is oval shaped and hard. I turn it over and see that it is a little bumblebee Christmas ornament. It has yellow and black stripes, light blue wings, and a little smile on his face. He is so cute.

"How much was he?" I ask.

"Don't worry about it. I want you to remember our little trip. Just the two of us." She gives me a little squeeze and smiles.

I carefully wrap up the ornament with the tissue paper and put it in my pocket. I make sure to zip the pocket so that it doesn't fall out. As soon as it is safe, we head back outside.

"This means you have to come on the bumblebee ride with me," I say, pointing up into the trees. There is a dark green metal rail that goes all around the park and little bumble bee cars hang from it. I want to go on it so that I can feel like I'm flying.

Mom looks up and her eyes narrow. "I don't like heights," she looks back at me.

I lower my arm and pull my mittens on. I try not to show how sad I am, but I can feel my ears getting hot and I know my face is turning red. I hope my eyes don't start to fill up with tears. I hate when they do that.

"If you promise to hold my hand the whole time, I will go on it with you Teester," Mom says.

I look up at her and smile. "Really?"

"Yeah, but I'm only doing it once." She holds one skinny finger up to emphasize her point.

"After that then we can go to the petting zoo?" I ask.

"Whatever you want. Today is your day." She holds out her hand to me.

I've never had my own day, with just Mom and me. Normally Mom is too busy with Emma or with running errands all day to take me places like this. I like being home alone sometimes, or with Dad, but being with Mom is different. I like feeling special. I like feeling important to Mom. I grab her hand and we walk towards the line for the Bumble Bee ride together.

At the front of the line there is a sign that is in the shape of a reindeer. The elf working there makes each kid stand next to the red nose before letting them on.

"You might be too short to ride this one, T." Mom says.

I watch a few kids get onto the ride and one little boy get turned away. He walks past me, with his head down, back towards the rest of the park. I don't want to be like him, too short to ride and then walk past all the other kids who are watching and laughing at him. I wiggle my toes and my wet socks make a little bit of a swishing sound.

Mom kneels down so she can look at my face. "When you get up to the line just stand as tall as you can and maybe even a little on your tiptoes," she whispers, "I'll try to distract the elf working it so he doesn't notice you're too little."

I nod. We're up next and I stand as tall as I can. I even point my nose in the air so that my head is tilted up.

"Sweetheart, can you stand next to Rudolph for me?" The elf has on green tights and a funny white outfit. He seems kind of bored as he scratches his head. His little green pointed hat with fake elf ears connected to it almost falls off, but he catches it just in time and smiles when he notices me watching him.

I walk to the sign, careful to stay on my tippy toes the whole time. Just as I stand under the red nose mom says, "How high does this ride go? I'm a little nervous of heights." She smiles at the elf. There seems to be something in her eyes, because she's blinking funny.

"Don't worry, it doesn't go that high and it goes pretty slow too so you have nothing to worry about." He smiles and tries to run his fingers through his hair, but his hat falls off. He leans down to get it and I notice his face turning pink.

It's hard to stand tall for this long while Mom talks with him, but I stay on my tiptoes until he looks back at me.

"You're going to have to help your mom on the ride, alright?" He motions for us to climb into the little bumble bee car. I run to the side of the yellow and black car and climb into the very front. Mom sits behind me and the worker pulls on the straps. "This is called a monorail. It's kind of like a train and will show you the whole park from up high in the trees." He helps buckle us in and smiles at Mom.

"Thanks for all your help," Mom says.

"You bet." He walks over to the control panel, pushes a green button and waves as we move past him.

The car moves out straight for a minute before angling up into the trees.

"Hold my hand! You promised!" Mom yells and reaches for me. A puff of mom's green apple shampoo fills the air around us.

Even though I am buckled to her, I hold her hand. The car moves higher and higher and Mom closes her eyes. I want to lean over the side of the car and look at the reindeer beneath us, but I hold onto Moms hand instead. Even then, I know that the intimacy between us is as fleeting as two palms touching, so I hold on as long as I can.

That Night

I'm sitting at the dinner table in the living room. It sits along the wall that is underneath the staircase. The small metal futon fills up the rest of the living room and sits right in front of the old bookcase that holds the TV and VCR. All the lights are on in the living room and the small kitchen next to it. I try to finish my spelling homework because tomorrow is the big test. If I do a good job, I could win the award for all fourth graders this week. But it's hard to concentrate because Mom is wide awake and cleaning, again.

"Mom, why are you scrubbing the walls like that?" I watch her. She is on her tippy toes with a dirty rag wiping the walls from the ceiling to the floor. Her grey shirt clings to her because she's sweaty. I notice that she has lost even more weight. When she turns around to look at me, I can see her collar bones and her face looks almost sharp in comparison to the usual rolls and double chin. Throughout the years her weight yo-yo's back and forth between obese and skinny. I will know that she is back to her old drug habit when she pulls out the box labeled "skinny clothes" and throw her old fat clothes away. But tonight, I just think about how her thin face and prominent chin kind of look like a witch and I wonder if that will be what she dresses up for in a few weeks for Halloween.

"Because they're nasty. Can't you see all the dirt?" She dips the rag back into her bowl of bleach water. I look at the wall and try to see the dirt. It just looks like a normal white wall to me.

"I don't see anything." I shake my head.

"Of course, you don't. Nobody ever sees the mess. But it's always there. Just starring at me." She scratches her face and looks around the room. Sometimes she cleans like this and says that she is just in a cleaning mood, but tonight she's doing it differently. She's doing weird things. Like the walls.

"Are you ok?" I watch her as she focuses on me. Her eyes narrow.

"I'm fine, Tara. Why don't you go to bed?" Her voice is deeper than normal, and I know she's mad.

"I'm not sleepy enough to sleep." I lie. I'm too embarrassed to tell her that my half-sister won't let me into the room we are supposed to share. And even if I told her about it, she would probably pick Emma's side over mine and make me sleep on the floor in the living room anyways. I don't think about it until years later, but Mom always joins a little team with Emma because she probably feels guilty. Guilty that Emma doesn't have her biological father in her life and guilty that she had another daughter, when Emma begged her not to.

"Then lay on the futon and watch TV until Dad comes home. Once he's here you'll have to go upstairs." Dad always sleeps on the couch. He says it's because he wants to be able to protect us from anything that might be on the deck like bears or strangers. I asked Mom about it once and she just told me to mind my own business. "Just lie down and be quiet. I have to clean. The dirt is just crawling out of the walls." She turns back to the bowl on the floor. Next to it there is a scrubber brush that I use on the dirty dishes. She dips it into the bowl, stands on a stool next to her and starts to scrub the ceiling.

I shrug and pull on the couch to make it flat. I quietly grab some blankets out of Finn's room and close the door, so he won't wake up. Turning on the TV I surf the channels until I find the carton channel. Just before I fall asleep Finn crawls into bed with me and I let him into my blanket. He squishes me and I know it's because he's cold and wants me to warm him up.

"Come on Finn, you're cold!" I try to get away from him but his toes follow me around the bed. He presses them against my legs and giggles. They feel like little ice cubes, but I don't really mind. He will warm up soon and I like being close to someone. "Let's watch a cartoon, ok?" I say.

He nods his head and I turn the volume up.

"Yes, I need an ambulance. I don't know what she's done. Yes, my wife. She's...she's not acting right. She was cleaning the house with all the lights on and I went to bed and then I woke up just now to go pee and I found her in the laundry room. No, she's just sitting there mumbling to herself. She hasn't spoken to me yet. Hold on." Dad's voice is soft and deep. I wonder why he is up so late. I remember when he came home and nudged me over to make room for him on the couch but that was hours ago.

I open my eyes and peek over my pillow. I don't want to get up in case Dad gets upset that I'm awake. All the lights are still on and Dad's standing in the kitchen. He's holding the phone to his chest and he looks upset.

"Natalie, can you talk to me?" He's leaning into the laundry room. His face is pale. "Natalie? What did you do? Can you tell me so I can help you?" His hand runs through his white hair.

"No, she's still mumbling. She's talking about heaven and Satan. She's crying and freaking out. No, she hasn't hurt me. I need an ambulance. Why do we have to wait for the Sheriff? Just hurry." Dad hangs up the phone and throws it onto the counter.

"Natalie the ambulance is coming ok? You're going to be ok." Dad's voice is shaking, and I think he might be crying. I watch his face for any signs of tears. After a minute I decide that he wouldn't ever cry. He's too tough. His voice must be shaking because he's scared.

"I let him in Heinrich. I told him to come into the house." Mom's yelling.

I look around the room for someone she let in. I'm scared until I don't see anyone, but I scoot next to Finn anyway and make sure that he's safe. I listen to Mom some more and can tell that she's crying because she is breathing funny and sniffing her nose.

"No one's in here but us." Dad's voice is loud and calm. He must be feeling a little better. The way he's talking makes me feel better, too.

"He's here. I don't really want to be here anymore. I don't want to live anymore."

"Natalie, stop. You're fine. Everything's going to be fine. There's no one in the house but us and the kids." I watch as he checks his watch. He makes a fist and hits the wall next to the doorway. I've never seen him like this. He's making me nervous.

"Is he hurting the kids? I need to check on them."

Dad stands in the doorway and I can see Mom trying to get into the kitchen. He pushes her back into the laundry room and blocks the door on each side with his arms.

"He's going to get the kids! Let me out!" Mom screams.

I look around the room expecting to see one of the villains from the cartoons lurking in the corner. I don't see anyone, but that doesn't make me feel any better. I slide my hand under the blanket and find Finn's. Wiggling my finger into his hand I make sure that he is safe. I scoot next to him so that if anyone does show up they will have to get past me first in order to get to him.

"No one is there. You're not going to go to the kids. Just sit down and wait for the ambulance," Dad straightens his shirt. I've never seen him this fidgety before. Seeing him play with his clothes and check his watch every few seconds makes things serious.

Finn rolls over in his sleep and I crouch down and cover his head up. Maybe if I cover him up he won't hear Mom yelling. I'm not sure what's going on, but I know something is wrong and I don't want Finn to be upset.

"Don't hurt the kids. They didn't do it. I let you in. Heinrich tell him it was my fault he's here."

"Natalie there is no one there." I peek over my pillow and watch as Dad paces the kitchen floor. He picks up the phone again.

"I called 10 minutes ago for my wife. I need the ambulance to get here now. It's taking too fucking long. No, she's just yelling and mumbling about Satan. How long is the sheriff going to take? Can you get him here faster?" he slams the phone back down.

"Don't go to the kids! I let you in." Mom screams. Finn wakes up and I feel him trying to crawl out of the blanket.

"Tara?" Finn tries to pull the blanket off his head. I open it just a little so I can see his face. It's a little sweaty and his big blue eyes are wide and still sleepy.

"Stay in there right now," I say.

"What's wrong?"

I shush him. I don't want Dad to hear us. "Mom's sick. Just lay back down or Dad's going to be mad that you're awake." I whisper into the blanket and pull it closed. Finn opens it a crack but stays inside. Mom is talking and Dad is on the phone again. I don't know why he wants an ambulance. I've never had one of them come to the house before. I think they are supposed to have their lights and sirens on the whole way and if they do they will wake up the whole neighborhood. I look at the VCR and see the green neon clock. It says it is 4:30 in the morning. I have never been awake this late before. I wish I felt more excited about being up and not so afraid. My stomach hurts and I hope the ambulance will help Mom soon.

"Go check on mom, T." Finn whispers to me after a few minutes.

"I will if you go back to sleep." Finn nods his head and closes his eyes.

I look over my pillow and see Dad looking at me. I duck my head down but he comes over anyways.

"Tara, why are you awake?"

"The lights woke me up," I lie. I don't want to tell him that he woke me up because he was on the phone. Dad walks over to the light switch and dims them.

"Go back to sleep."

"Dad, is Mom ok?" I whisper. He freezes for a second and then leans down.

"No. She is really sick and I have to bring her to the hospital. Can you make sure that Finn doesn't wake up? Can you take care of him for me?"

"Is Mom going to get better?" I ask. He looks towards the kitchen where the door to the laundry room is.

"I don't know. Just lay down." The way he says it makes me tremble. I hold onto Finn and close my eyes. I've never prayed before, but I whisper to God now. I hope he hears me.

Dad walks back into the kitchen and crouches down by the door. Mom is still crying and talking. But I can't hear what she is saying now. I hope she is feeling better.

After a while I can hear something on the deck. I don't know what it is but it sounds big. I hope it's not a bear. I look over into the kitchen and Dad is leaning on the sink with his back to me. The thing on the deck moves again and I get up. Tiptoeing through the living room I sneak into the kitchen. Just as I pass the laundry room door I decided not to look. I don't want to see Mom sick.

"Dad?" I whisper.

He turns around so fast he knocks into me. "What are you doing?" he grabs my shoulders and holds me close. So close that it feels like he is hugging me. Maybe he wanted to make sure I wouldn't fall down, but as I write this I wonder if he was trying to shield me from seeing Mom that night.

"There's something on the deck. I don't know what but it sounds big."

"Ok, let's go look." He takes my shoulders and starts pushing me into the living room. I can't help it and I peak into the laundry room. Mom is sitting on the floor. Her thick curls look wet and hang down around her shoulders. She is looking at her hands and whispering to them as they shake. Scratch marks cover her arms and her skin is pale. Dad pulls me away from the door quickly and sits me down on the couch. He looks through the front window before unlocking the door.

"I need to talk with the Sheriff, can you lay back down?" He runs his hands through his hair and grabs his glasses off the table.

"Why is the Sheriff here?" I ask. I like the Sheriffs. They come to school sometimes and teach us about how to be safe. One of them even let me hold his handcuffs once.

"Tara, I will explain everything to you later but right now I need you to lie down and stay quiet, ok?"

I nod. There is a knock at the door and Dad opens it. They talk with each other in low voices and Dad brings him into the laundry room.

"Natalie, can you talk with me?" The Sheriff's voice is loud. He sounds tough, kind of like the old cowboy movies we watch. "Can you tell me what day it is? Or who the president is?"

Mom is talking again. I hope she is answering his questions. I peak inside of the blanket to make sure Finn is asleep. He isn't. He stares back at me and I know he's scared. I smile and grab his small hand. Even though he's five years old and in the first grade, his hand is still kind of small and I like how it fits into my own.

"Can I talk with you in your living room?" The sheriff is motioning for Dad to follow him. I close my eyes so he doesn't see that I'm awake.

"We're going to bring her to the hospital and check her out. Has she had a history of drug use?" I open my eyes slowly and watch the Sherriff take out a small notepad and pen from his pocket.

"Yes, but when I find out that she's on drugs I make her stop. She hasn't done any for a while now." Dad takes a deep breath. He looks tired.

"Has she seemed depressed lately?"

"Not that I know of."

"Well I am going to be honest with you. I think she tried to kill herself with a bunch of drugs. I found a soda can and lighter and it looks like she was using it as a pipe. I'm not sure what the effects will be, but because I think she is a danger to herself and possibly you and the kids I'm going to request her to be held for at least 72 hours to be evaluated. I hope that this is just a bad trip, but you never know with drugs."

Dad nods his head and takes the Sheriff back to Mom. I guess Mom must have tripped and hurt herself somehow. I pull the blanket off of Finn and squeeze his hand.

"Mom just tripped. That's what the cop said. But she's going to the doctor and will be ok."

He smiles and peaks over at the cop. "He has a cool belt. I wonder what's in the pockets. I bet he has bullets. And dog treats for the cop dogs."

Finn keeps whispering about the cop until the paramedics come in. They go straight to the laundry room and check on Mom. I'm happy they are here because maybe they will be able to make Mom feel better.

"I want to see the kids. You know, I've got to make sure that he hasn't hurt them." Mom is standing in the kitchen looking at the couch. I push Finn down and try to keep still. There is something wrong with Mom's face. Her eyes look different and make me want to hide. Her skin is yellow and covered in thin scratches from her ragged nails. I pull the blanket over Finn and up to my chin. Finn gets still, and I know he is pretending to be asleep too.

Dad comes and sits on the futon with me. "Tester, Mom wants to say goodbye before going to the doctors." He shakes my shoulder and I open my eyes slow, so he thinks I was sleep. "Sweetheart, Mom is going to the doctor. Say goodbye, ok?"

The Sherriff holds onto Mom's shoulders and guides her into the living room. I sit up and smile at her. Her hair must have dried and is frizzy. It spreads out behind her like when spider webs blow in the wind. She's wearing the same clothes as when I went to bed, but now she has a grey blanket wrapped around her shoulders.

"Tara, I'm so sorry I let him in. Don't talk to him, alright? He lies about everything. Just keep Finn safe."

The sheriff starts to pull her away.

"No, not yet. Where's my buddy?" Mom looks around wildly. I pull down the covers and Finn rolls over.

"Finn wake up." I poke his stomach until he opens his eyes. He smiles a little and I know that he's proud of himself for pretending to be asleep for so long.

"Mom is leaving and she wants to say bye." I point over to where Mom is standing behind the couch.

"Where're you going?" He rubs his face and crawls to the edge of the couch. Mom tries to go to him, but the sheriff keeps her away. She struggles for a second but then her shoulders go limp and she starts to cry.

"You're a good boy, don't let him tell you anything else. Don't let him hurt you. I love you buddy."

"Who's going to hurt me?" Finn asks as he looks around the living room. There are a few paramedics in the room and Finn stares at each of them before looking back at mom.

"Satan. He's here. I let him in. I'm so sorry buddy. I'm so sorry I let him in." She looks up at the ceiling and scratches her face until a thin line of blood drips down it.

"Mom, it'll be alright." I smile at her, but she just pulls at her hair and cries harder.

I watch as the sheriff pulls her out of the door and across the deck. I can hear her yelling and I hope she doesn't get in trouble for doing that to a cop.

"Tara, I need you to watch Finn. I have to go down and talk to the paramedics to see where they are taking your mom. Everything is going to be fine. I promise." He kisses my forehead, ruffles Finn's hair and goes outside.

"T, who's going to hurt me?" Finn looks scared. He snuggles up next to me and I put my arm around him.

"No one. Let's watch something ok?"

"Can we watch *Home Alone?*" He asks.

I smile and nod my head. I put the movie in the VCR and push play. *Home Alone* starts and hopefully it makes Finn feel better. I crawl back onto the futon and pull him close. My heart feels like a bird locked in a cage and I hope Finn can't feel it through my shirt. I don't like what Mom was saying about Satan being in the house. I will ask Dad to leave all the lights on when he comes back inside.

I think about what the Sherriff said. I don't know why anyone would want to kill themselves, but especially Mom. I feel like it might be my fault. I try to think of all the things I could have done to make her feel like she didn't want to be here with us anymore. I know I like to fight with Emma and I know that I can be a big brat. Maybe it is my fault. My fingers are tingly, and I know I need to calm down, for Finn's sake. He can always tell when I'm upset and he's watching me carefully right now. I take a deep breath and pull the blanket up over my shoulders. Finn is warm, and the movie is funny and soon I feel relaxed as I hold him tight, so nothing can hurt him.

21 Weeks

Before going down to find out the gender of the twins, I put on a black shirt and try not to be too nervous. All the women and mothers at church or the post office or really anywhere I run into them have been asking if I can sense what genders they're going to be. "If they are sitting high up in your belly, they're definitely girls" an ancient woman in the pew behind me whispers before Sacrament meeting starts. Her face is cracked so much it looks like the old bark on the ancient oak tree near the house I grew up in.

"If you really like spicy food, at least one is a girl. I can't believe they're two in there!" a mother of six boys tells me as she restrains two of her boys at once. "Oh, I hope you have a girl. I've always wanted one." She runs after a few more of her boys as they start sword fighting in the isles of Stater Brothers. I turn around quickly and retreat from them before she can come back.

"Tara, we're going to be late." Alex calls from the bathroom. I pull on my shirt one last time, trying to make sure it covers my growing stomach, and run out to meet him.

He's wearing a bright yellow shirt and I like how it makes his blue eyes shine. He holds my hand to stop me from fidgeting and smiles.

"Ready to see what we're having?"

"I don't know. I'm a little nervous."

"Don't be."

We walk to the car in silence and drive down Highway 18 listening to the oldies station. There is no smog or clouds and I can see the entire city of San Bernardino below us. The grid looks like someone carefully planned out the city, something that is lost when driving through the poor and unkempt streets themselves. Further out there is a bright orange strip that gleams. As always when seeing the ocean from this far away, my breath is taken away. Catalina Island raises up out of the orange and red water and looks beautiful.

After just two turns the view disappears between the cliffs of the mountain and I'm brought back to reality. I look at my stomach and hold onto it. I press down just a little and can feel a few lumps inside. I have no idea if I'm feeling a leg or a bum, or if I'm feeling some parts of one baby and some of the other, but I don't care. I feel a little better knowing that they are going through all of this with me.

The rest of the drive is uneventful and before I'm ready we are walking into the x-ray and sonogram office in the basement of my doctor's office. Alex checks in for us while I sit and fiddle with my wedding ring.

He walks back to me and hold my hand while we wait.

"Cummins?" a nurse dressed all in pink calls from the doorway.

"Have fun, see you in a second." Alex kisses me and I walk to meet her.

"Ready to see your little ones?" She smiles and her blonde bob sways a little.

"Let's do it," I say, with much more enthusiasm in my voice then I feel.

The room is the same as last time. I change into a gown and lay on the cold table. She covers me up with a sheet and squirts the blue jelly onto my tummy before we start the ultrasound.

"How far are you now?"

"21 weeks."

"Would you like me to tell you the gender if I catch a peak, or wait for your husband to come in?"

"Could we wait for Alex?"

"Sure."

Silence fall between us and I close my eyes. It's actually relaxing until she presses hard and the babies squirm. Before long Alex is called in and we hold hands while she puts on a fresh pair of gloves.

"They are both growing just fine. Nothing to worry about. Heartbeats are in the right range and just 2 beats off each other. Now, I didn't see any private parts earlier, so let's see if they will show us."

She turns the screen towards us, and we see the little babies. This time, they actually look like babies instead of skeletal aliens. The ultrasound tech shows us each body part and lets us see the heart beating on the first baby before trying to see the sex.

"Well, this one isn't shy at all. Just flashed us right away. You see those little ridges? That means she is a girl!"

I look up at Alex's face and can see his happiness. I know he must be thinking about his three nieces and how much he loves them. He's going to be great with his daughter. I smile and think about how cute little dresses and bows will be. I don't really know how to do hair very well, since I was such a tomboy, but I bet I will learn.

"Now, let's try to see baby b's sex." The tech moves the wand higher up on my stomach and the baby immediately starts to squirm away from it.

"Oh, what a rascal! It just rolled right up in a ball! The entire time I was measuring its sister this baby was stretching out and throwing its feet and hands in the way. How funny it rolls up in a ball when I want to check its gender." She giggles and pushes down a little harder.

After almost 10 minutes of trying the tech sets down the wand. "We may need to wait until next time to see."

I try to hide my disappointment, but I know that Alex can tell. He squeezes my hand. I must not have hidden my sadness well because the technician smiles and says, "Well maybe I can try just one more time."

She puts a little more jelly on my stomach and quickly corners the baby up near my ribcage.

"And I got a glimpse, but I want to make sure…" She presses down a few more times, clicks a button on the big keyboard and smiles, triumphantly.

"And if you look on the screen, there is the little girl parts of your second daughter. Congrats Mom and Dad." She smiles.

I wipe the goo off my stomach and pull my pants back on under my gown. The technician leaves the room to us and Alex just stares at the picture of the girls that were printed out.

"So, two girls." I say.

"Yeah." His voice sounds wispy and I can tell he is beyond happy about the girls. "You happy, babe?"

"Yeah. I mean, I don't know how to do girl things and I feel a little overwhelmed. I'm used to taking care of Finn."

"What girl things?"

"Like hair and makeup." I pull my shirt on.

"That won't matter for a while and when it does, I'm sure you'll learn."

"I hope so. Maybe you can teach me since you have three nieces already and they adore you."

"I don't do their hair. I just pinch them and push them down and chase them around."

I look at him to see if he is joking, but he's not. I laugh, and my nerves seems to melt away.

"You're right. Everything will be fine with the girls." I say. I repeat that to myself over a few times, trying to convince myself that it is true.

Aftermath

The next morning, I wake up to the smell of eggs and bacon burning. I roll over and am surprised to see my godmother Charlotte in the kitchen. Her short black hair is straight and sits right above her shoulders and her thin body moves around the small kitchen quickly. She sings a song and plates the food before she notices me watching her.

"Good morning Tara. Want some breakfast?"

Grey smoke spirals up from the frying pan and the smell hurts my nose. I don't want to be rude so I nod my head and sit at the table. She pours a glass of orange juice and sets it next to my plate. We never have orange juice, because it's so expensive, so I drink it first. The sweet and tangy flavor helps to mask the burnt flavor of the rest of the food. I eat quickly and then I get dressed.

"Brush your teeth, comb your hair and then we will have a morning prayer before school." She walks over to the couch and wakes Finn up. He is cranky and she has to pull him out of the bed for him to finally get up.

"Where's Dad?" I ask, sneaking a piece of lightly burnt bacon from Finn's plate.

"He went down the hill to check on your mom. He asked me to get you ready this morning and to drop you off at the bus."

"Is mom ok?" Finn asks, shoving a huge spoon of egg into his mouth.

"I'm not sure. We can pray for her if you want." Charlotte grabs herself a plate and sits next to Finn.

I go into the bathroom and brush my hair. I don't remember Mom feeling sick and I feel like it was something more than just tripping and falling over. I remember the strange look in her eye and how she was yelling about Satan. I won't be able to pick out the signs of an overdose for several more years, but the feeling that something is wrong is the same. It feels like something heavy is on my shoulders and inside of my chest. I put the brush down and grab my toothbrush. After just a few quick scrubs I spit the toothpaste gunk into the sink, rinse my mouth out and go look for my backpack.

I notice my spelling homework, abandoned on the table, and shove it into my bag. Hopefully I can do well on the test today.

"Tara, lets pray before we leave." Charlotte motions for me to sit on the couch with her and Finn. I sit, awkwardly, and fold my arms. Praying is not something that we ever do as a family or on our own. We go to church, but just because Charlotte picks us up and drops us back off after it's done. I think church is fun but praying always makes me feel a little weird. Charlotte closes her eyes and takes a deep breath.

"Dear God, thank you for our lives, this day and our breakfast. Please watch over Natalie and heal her. Let her come home to her children better then when she left. Please let us be better today than we were yesterday. Our lives are yours, do with them as you will. Amen." She opens her eyes and smiles at me. "What do you have to do in school today?"

"I have a spelling test, but I didn't get to finish my homework. I will probably do pretty bad."

"Can I help quiz you while we drive?"

"Sure." I hand her my list of words and she reads over it a few times.

"How about I drive you all the way to school, so we have more time to practice?"

Mom never drives us to school, and Dad can't since he has work. I've always wanted to know what it was like to be dropped off right in front of the school. Everyone would be watching and I would be able to brag about it to my friends. I smile and nod.

After school Dad picks me up at the bus stop. Finn is in the back munching on some snacks, so I throw my backpack at him. It hits him right in the face and knocks him over. As he scrambles to sit back up, I steal his chips and shove a few of them into my mouth before Dad hands them back to him.

"We're going down to the hospital to see Mom. I need you to behave yourselves and not fight, got it?" He raises his eyebrows at me.

"Yeah, I'll be good." I raise my hands in surrender and he smiles for a second before he looks serious again. His eyes are red. I know he hasn't slept well.

The drive down the mountain is slow and I like it that way. I like looking out over the cliff and seeing the rocks and trees and the city way below us. I wonder how the trees grow on the side of the rocks without any dirt. Their dark brown roots stand out against the light grey stone that makes up the mountain. I look out of my window and up the side of the mountain next to us. There are lots of trees there, too. I hope they have strong roots, so they don't fall out.

Once we hit the streets in San Bernardino Dad takes a few turns and goes into a direction that I have never been in. After a few more turns I'm completely lost and stare out of the window. The streets are dirty and filled with potholes. Women stand on the street and are wearing pretty dresses. I wonder who they are waiting to pick them up.

"Teester, lock your door for me." Dad says.

I lock the door. I like watching the people on the street walk around and ride their bikes. Some of them look a little scary so I'm happy dad made me lock the door.

"We almost there?" I ask.

"Uh, I've never been to this hospital so I'm not sure. I think it's just a few streets away."

He turns into a dead end and has to make a U-turn. There is a tent set up in the alley behind a few of the buildings. It's dirty and has a few shirts hanging up on the top of it drying in the sun.

"People camp there?" I ask.

"No, they live there."

"Like, that's their only house?" Finn asks from the back seat. I turn to look at him and his eyes are wide.

"Yeah, they're homeless and live in the tent." Dad looks over at me and reaches for my hand. I look back at the tent in the alley and feel sad that whoever lives there doesn't have anywhere else to go.

After another five minutes Dad pulls into a weird driveway with a gate. Before we do anything to open it, the gate swings in on its own. We park into the open spot right in front and pile out. I grab Finn's hand and we follow Dad into the front doors.

There is a desk right inside of the front doors and a nurse in a pink shirt smiles at us. Behind her are a row of wheelchairs.

Finn points at them and without a word I know he wants to play with them. It would be fun to ride around in one for a while. Maybe, if the nurse goes away we can sneak one. I wiggle my eyebrows at him, letting him know that we will play with them just as soon as I can manage it.

"My wife was brought here this morning from the ER. I need to check on her."

"Name?"

"Natalie Muller."

"There is actually a note here that the physician wants to speak with you before you go back to her room. If you wait in the room to your right," she points to a large room with blue couches and chairs and a big isle in the middle, "I will call him, and he will be out as soon as he can."

Dad's eyebrows furrow and make him look mad, but I know he's just worried. He nods and walks into the room. I pull Finn along and we sit on one of the blue couches.

"See those wheel chairs?" I whisper to Finn.

He nods.

"If Dad goes to talk to the doctor and the nurse goes away we can grab one."

"And race?" his six-year-old voice is too loud for a whisper.

"Shh, dummy!" I say, looking at Dad to make sure he didn't hear us. I'm know that this is exactly the thing Dad would say is misbehaving and I promised him I would be good. But if we just do a few races then put it all back, no one will know.

"Muller ?" A man in a white coat calls from a doorway.

Dad stands up, "Yes?"

The doctor walks over to us and sits down. His hair is grey and he wears big round glasses that make his eyes look bigger than normal. He has lots of pens in his front pocket and a big folder in his hands. He opens it, looks at the paper and then nods slowly.

"Sorry to have to meet under these circumstances," his voice is quite and sounds like someone is pinching his nose.

"How is she?"

"In the emergency room last night, they had to sedate her because of her behavior. They ran a lot of test and found a lot of different drugs in her system. She hasn't woken up since we transported her here. I was going to try to wake her right before you came."

"I'd like to be there when she wakes up."

"I don't know if that is the best idea, sir."

"She's my wife. I will be there." Dad's voice gets louder and the doctor squirms in his seat a little.

"I would highly advise against it. People who suffer from an overdose like this often have many psychological problems if they survive. The woman you knew is not going to be the one who wakes up in the room today."

"And that's for certain?" Dad looks over at me and Finn and tries to smile but can't. Instead he reaches out for my hand, "We have young kids who need their Mom," Dad whispers.

"In most of the cases I have seen, they are a different person when they wake up. I've been doing this for thirty-seven years. I'm sorry."

Dad's shoulders slump. I squeeze his hand.

"What would you suggest then?" Dad's voice sounds angry.

"Call a lawyer and get the divorce working. When she wakes up she will need a lot of treatment and again, will most likely be a completely different person."

"Where would she live? Who would care for her?"

"I don't know, you guys would have to figure that out. But for the best interest of the rest of the family I would suggest separating."

I think about the tent in the alley and how people are without homes. If Dad and Mom get divorced, then Mom won't have a home. I don't want to see her in a tent without anything nice. I don't want Mom to go away. I look at Finn and his eyes are almost as big as the doctors because I know he is scared.

"Dad, I just want Mom to wake up. I don't care if she's a little different." I say, not fully understanding the situation.

He looks up at me and nods his head. "Can we go wake her up?"

"I would prefer the children to stay here. There are books and I'm sure the nurse will keep an eye on them."

"I want to see Mom!" Finn cries.

"Doodle Bug, I'll bring you to see Mom after she wakes up, alright?" Dad says.

The doctor takes a deep breath but doesn't say anything. I don't know why he doesn't want us to see Mom.

Dad looks at me and I smile. "I'll be good and watch Finn."

He scratches my back for a minute before following the doctor behind a door. As soon as it closes I turn to Finn and smile.

"What?"

"The nurse just left, and Dad left too." I look at him then look at the line of wheelchairs and back at him. I raise my eyebrows and wiggle them.

"Really?" he whispers.

"Let's go!"

We run to the wheelchairs and each choose one. Mine is blue and has silver wheels. I pull it out of the line and sit in it. I don't know how to roll around with it, so I just scoot with my feet towards Finn. His wheelchair is brown and has a big metal rail on the back with hooks, probably for coats and stuff.

"How do we make them move?" He yells.

"Just come sit in mine and I'll push you."

He runs over to me and jumps into my chair. I grab the handles on the back and push him slowly. The wheels roll easily, and he laughs. I look around the empty room and the long isle in the middle.

I turn Finn around at the end of it and start to make the sound of an engine.

"What're you doing?" He turns to look at me.

"You better hold on!" I yell and start to run. He turns back around and grabs the handles. His curly hair stands up because we are going so fast. We both laugh until I get through the room and have to turn around again.

"Do it again!" He says, turning back to me.

"Ok, but hold on." I look to the end of the isle and see a big blue couch against the wall. If I run fast enough and let go right at the end Finn will probably crash into the couch. I smile and rev my engine again.

"Are you ready?" I ask.

Finn looks back at me and stops smiling. "What're you going to do?"

"Get set!" I say, pulling the wheelchair backwards a little.

"Tara?" He asks.

He must see how excited I am, but before he can tell me to stop I start to run. I run as fast as I can. He screams and holds on. Just at the spot I normally start to slow down, I let go of the handles and laugh.

Finn looks back at me for a second before turning around again. When the wheelchair hits the couch, he flies out of it and hits the wall above the couch. He falls into the soft cushions and glares at me.

I run to him and pull him up.

"You ok?" I say, between laughing.

"No." He slaps my hand away from him.

"Come on, that was fun! You flew!" I can't stop laughing and it's hard to breathe.

"I hit the wall."

"Yeah, but that was awesome." I push him a little until he smiles.

"How high did I go?" he asks.

We look at the wall and see a little dent halfway up it. I point and we both laugh until we can't breathe.

A door opens next to us and Dad comes out with the same doctor as before.

"You guys ok?" He asks.

"Yeah."

"Mom has been awake for a little while. She even ate something when I was back there." He rubs his chin and his white whiskers make a scratchy sound.

"Can we go see her?" I ask.

"Yeah, they're setting her up in a visitor's room. Let's go." He picks Finn up and carries him into the back. I grab his back pocket, so I don't get lost.

The white halls are bright, and the lights make it even worse. My eyes hurt a little as we follow the doctor to a back room. Before opening the door, he turns to us.

"This is not a good idea. She is not responding to anything right now. I don't want to terrify, and potentially scar the children." He says quietly to Dad.

"If she seems them, she's got to recognize them."

The doctor shakes his head and goes into the room. Before we follow, Dad turns to me and bends down so the three of our faces are next to each other.

"Tara, Finn. I need you to be brave. Mom is sick. She doesn't know who I am right now. She looks weird too. But it's still Mom. I want you to try to talk to her for a minute. I'm sure she will know you guys and start to get better if she hears you and sees you, alright?" He looks at each of us and Finn nods.

"Ok Dad, we'll be brave."

We walk into the room together. The lights are different in the room. They aren't as bight and the yellow walls are a little weird. They have bubbles on them that look like they are made with pillows. In the middle of the room is a highchair big enough for Mom to be sitting in it. Her arms and legs are strapped in with yellow straps. Her hair is all flat on one side, and poufy on the other like she slept funny. Her skin matches the yellow straps and she's wearing a weird white outfit. She is staring up at the ceiling and some drool is coming out of her mouth.

I look up at Dad and he takes a deep breath. Finn buries his face into Dad's neck and doesn't say anything. I walk towards Mom and only stop when the doctor holds out his hands.

"This is as close as you can get, alright?" he says.

"Mom?" I ask.

She doesn't do anything when I say her name.

"Mom, it's Tara." I say.

Mom's face tilts down towards mine, slowly. Her eyes are wide and unseeing. Then she slams her head down onto the little tray and starts to scream. Her head slams onto the tray over and over while her screams echo in the small room. Dad picks me up, juggling Finn and me both, and we leave Mom with the doctors. Rhythmic thuds and echoes of screams follow us to the entrance. Dad doesn't stop walking until we are in the car. He buckles Finn up and gives him a kiss.

"Let's go get dinner, just the three of us alright?" He says, ruffling Finn's hair.

"Anywhere we want to go?" I ask. I try to sound happy.

"Anywhere you want." He says, holding my hand.

"Del Taco? And can we eat inside?" Finn says, quietly from the back.

"Sure thing, buddy. You can get whatever you want to."

I turn to look at Finn and he smiles. The three of us hold hands and we fly down the freeway together.

25 Weeks

I shove another pillow in-between my knees and try to go back to sleep. I clench my eyes shut and try to think of nothing. But soon the weight of my belly and the babies pulls my back into a strange angle. I try to ignore the pressure while watching the tree branches tickle the window. The light from the moon cast eerie shadows onto the bed. Even laying down breathing is difficult because the twins are pushing everything out of the way, including my lungs, so that they can continue to grow. I trace the shadows lightly with my finger and listen to the soft cricket songs wishing they would sweep me away.

I sigh and push myself slowly up. It takes me almost an entire minute to be fully seated. I take several deep breaths and wait for my heart to stop pounding. It feels like I just ran up a set of bleachers. Scooting over to the edge of the bed I realize there is no way that I'm going to be able to sleep right now. Will the rest of the pregnancy be like this? I can't imagine going another fifteen weeks like this.

I climb out of bed and quietly walk through the cabin. The chilly air feels soothing. I look down at my belly and feel frustrated. Frustrated that my entire body aches all the time. Frustrated that I can't sleep, or eat, or sit, or really do anything comfortably anymore.

And then I feel guilty. Being a mom is such an amazing thing. Something that not every woman gets a chance to be a part of. Shouldn't I be enjoying every part of being pregnant? What is wrong with me?

I turn around and my belly knocks over one of the high-chairs. It topples into the other one and they both end up in a heap on the kitchen floor. I don't even try to pick them up. I know I won't be able to reach them or stand up without assistance if I tried.

"Really? You keep me up all night, my belly is itchy and heavy and hurts, and now it is so big that its knocking things over?" I glare at my stomach. A part of me realizes that I'm ex-tremely tired and a bit irrational, but I don't care. I keep glaring at my stomach and letting my frustrations out. "You guys are always in the way. I can't turn around without bumping into something. I can't walk more than 2 minutes without being out of breath. I have never weighed this much before in my life. I have to have thirty pillows all around me to support my belly, and back, and legs, and arms just to sleep for an hour at a time before I have to pee again. You guys suck." I yell the last bit and let the echoes ring throughout the house.

"Tara? What's going on?" Alex stumbles from the bed-room. He rubs his eyes and reaches out for me.

"Nothing." I say, walking past him and collapsing onto the couch.

"Babe, seriously what is going on?" Alex lays down on the couch next to me.

"I just… I just don't want to be pregnant." I whisper. The horrible truth comes out and I feel like it's crushing me. Alex is not going to want to be around me anymore. He will know how I'm a terrible mother already.

"I wouldn't want to be pregnant either."

I look at him, surprised. He shrugs.

"It seems terrible."

"It is pretty terrible." I say. "You're not mad?"

He lays his head onto my lap. "Why would I be mad?"

"Because I'm already the worst mom."

He reaches for me and squeezes my hand. "Why would you say that?"

I look at our intertwined hands, terrified that he will realize he made some mistake in choosing me to be the mother of his children. "I don't have any of the… I don't know. The ingredients."

Alex looks confused. "Ingredients? For what?"

"For being a good mom."

He smiles, sleepily, "Mother's ingredients?"

"Yes. I don't have them. At least any of the good ones. I really am a bad mom already."

"You're not. You're growing two people at once. You're absolutely amazing."

"I yelled at them tonight just for being in there."

"They're fine. I could never do what you are doing, and not just because I don't have the right equipment." He smiles. "You're already the best mother. Don't worry so much." He rubs small circles onto my belly.

I wonder how well a baby in utero can hear. Can they feel my uneasiness? Did they hear my frustration and anger? Do they know how uneasy I am about becoming a mother?

Alex's hand moves slower and slower until it stops. I look down and realize that he is back asleep.

"Your daddy can fall asleep faster than anybody I know." I tap my belly. "He's going to be the best dad ever. He's already planning on when he can teach you soccer."

I tell the girls all about Alex and his family. I explain that they already have cousins who are dying to hold them. I whisper for so long my throat starts to hurt.

"I promise to always try. I may not be the best mom, but I will try. I love you, nuggets." I put my hands onto either side of my stomach and press just a little.

At the exact same time I feel something hit each of my palms. I take a deep breath and take my hands away from my stomach. I watch it for any movement.

"Was that really you, girls?" I ask.

I put my hands on my stomach again and again feel them each kick me.

"You're getting so strong! It's actually a little creepy how hard you just hit me!" They do it again.

"Do you like my voice?" Kicks.

"Do you want me to sing you a lullaby?" Kicks.

I try to think of any lullaby, but nothing comes to mind.

"This isn't a lullaby, exactly. But I'll sing to you anyways." I take a deep breath and sing "Kookaburra sits in the old gum-tree. Merry, merry king of the bush is he. Laugh, Kookaburra. Laugh. Kookaburra, gay your life must be."

My stomach feels like the twins are dancing. They have never been this active before. Instead of focusing on how strange it is, I soak up every moment. They're strong. They're healthy. They're my sweet little girls.

We sing and dance the night away.

Don't Cry

After school, I run into the room that I share with my sister. I throw the first progress report from middle school down onto the bed and look around on the floor. Underneath some clothes I can just see the corner. There it is. The book. She brought it home a month ago and had thrown it on the floor. I know that I shouldn't touch her stuff, but the book looks good and I haven't been able to go to the library in a while. I take *Harry Potter and the Sorcerer's Stone* down into the living room. Grabbing a blanket, I cuddle up on the old brown couch. I open the book to the first page.

Reading for hours at a time always makes my neck hurt so I stand to stretch for a minute. I walk into the tiny kitchen and grab a glass of water. I drink it at the sink and then run back to the couch. The book is warm from where my hands have been, and I turn to page 116 and keep reading. After a minute I hear something on the deck.

I stop and listen. It sounds like someone is walking outside. Just as I turn to look through the main window, Emma walks through the door. I know that if she sees me with her book I will get into trouble. I tilt the book, hoping she won't notice the cover.

"You're so weird reading all the time. Is that all you ever do?" she asks, and walks past me into the kitchen. I watch her grab a bag of chips from on top of the refrigerator, a soda from the box on the floor and a candy bar from the freezer.

"I guess books are all you have since you're such a loser." She laughs at me as she walks up the narrow staircase to our room.

I smile because she didn't notice the book. I take a deep breath and read more. *"A horrible thought struck Harry, as horrible thoughts always do when you're very nervous. What if he wasn't chosen at all? What if he just sat there with the hat over his eyes for ages, until professor McGonagall jerked it off his head and said there had obviously been a mistake and he'd better get back on the train?"*

I hope Harry will get into a house. Not fitting in is not fun. Especially when you're at home. And since Hogwarts is his home now, I hope he gets into the best house. If I was to go to Hogwarts, I would want to be in Gryffindor. Living in the house known for being courageous sounds like a good spot to me. I'm so nervous for Harry that I skip a few lines until his name is called.

"The last thing Harry saw before the hat dropped over his eyes was the hall full of people craning to get a good look at him. Next second he was looking at the black inside of the hat. He waited. 'Hmmm', said a small voice in his..."

The book flies out of my hand.

Emma is standing above me. "I told you not to touch my stuff."

I can't believe I didn't hear her coming down the stairs. Generally, they creek because she's fat. I have never heard her walk quietly before.

"But you don't even read." I watch as she raises her hand.

Slap.

My cheek stings and feels hot all over.

"Get out of here." She whispers, and I'm too scared to do anything else.

I run through the kitchen into the laundry room and open the sliding glass door. I run to the back of our yard and sit in the dirt. My cat, Tabby Sue, finds me and lays in my lap. I draw swirls in the dust and cry. I wish someone would show up at my door and whisk me away to a magical school where you get to live with people that are just like you. Then maybe I would fit in.

"Tara, time for dinner." Dad calls from the back door.

I roll over and rub my face. I didn't mean to fall asleep. I wipe dirt off of my clothes and hear Dad's heavy footsteps coming to find me.

"Teester, what're you doing out here?"

"I feel asleep with Tabby Sue." I look down and scratch Tabby's ears. He's still in my lap. He stretches and starts to purr.

"Why is your face so dirty?"

I don't know what to say. I don't feel like talking about what happened. I look down and rub the soft fur right behind Tabby's ears.

Grabbing my hands, Dad sits down next to me. His hands are big and rough from working, but they're warm too and I like them.

"What happened?"

I take a deep breath. "Emma slapped me."

"What'd you do?"

"I was just reading her Harry Potter book."

"No, I mean what did you do about her slapping you?"

"What do you mean?"

"Did you hit her back?"

"No, I cried."

Dad lets go of my hands. "You shouldn't cry, T. You should've hit her back."

I look up, surprised. Dad is always yelling at us to stop fighting. He hates when we yell, and he gets really mad if we slam doors.

"Crying shows weakness. It shows people that they can bully you. You've got to hurt them back. Hurt them so much that they don't mess with you again."

"But I don't want to fight."

"You know what happened to me when I didn't fight back when I was a kid?"

I shake my head. Dad doesn't like to talk about when he was little. Being in Germany was hard and when he came to California it was sometimes even worse.

"I came home from school with a bloody nose. Some kids at school hit me because I had a German accent and didn't know English very well. I was probably 11, so about a year younger than you. When I got home, and my dad saw my nose and he asked, 'Did you hit them back' and I said no. So, he rolled up his sleeves and beat me for a while. After he was done he told me to never come home like that again or he would beat me twice as bad. I never came home without fighting back after that."

"So, you always hurt them more?" I ask, looking into his face. His big blue eyes loose their characteristic twinkle.

"I'll tell you another story. In high school a girl asked me for help on some homework. Her football player boyfriend didn't like it. So, after school a group of his football buddies and he came up to me. I was standing under the flag waiting for my sister. He told me to stay away from his girl and I told him to fuck off and I turned to walk home, and he slammed my head into the flagpole. I woke up on the ground with that jackass right in front of me laughing with his friends. I stood up and ran at him. There was a chain link fence near us, so I pushed him into it. I grabbed the back of his head and rubbed his face into the fence like you would cheese on a grater. He was screaming and bleeding, but he couldn't get away, so I punched him with my other hand as hard as I could in his ribs, too, until his friend pulled me off. Then I kicked his buddy between the legs and he dropped. I turned back to the first guy and saw that his football lettermen jacket was covered in blood and his face was shredded. He was lying on the ground, so I started to kick him and kept kicking him until the police pulled me off. The kid was in the hospital for a few days and no one ever messed with me again."

The idea of my dad fighting is a scary one. He is strong and tall, his voice loud and deep when angry. I would never want to face him in a fight. The times I have seen him truly angry have scared me even though his anger was never aimed at me.

"Didn't you get hurt?" I ask.

"Yeah, I broke my jaw and we didn't have any money to go to the hospital. That's why it clicks. Feel." He pulls my hand up to his face. His cheek is covered in tiny hairs that are prickly. He closes his mouth and pretends to chew, and I can feel something clicking kind of like when I open and close my pencil box. I can hear his jaw pop each time, too.

"Do you understand?"

I scratch Tabby's ears and think.

"They won't hurt you if you hurt them too," I say.

"That's right. I need you to be strong. Next time Emma hits you, you hit her back and make sure it hurts."

I nod. He stands up and pulls me up with him.

Emma's face is sweaty, red and right in front of mine. I had been eating some chips before she took the whole bag away from me. I told her to give them back, but she just kept eating them. I know I have to be strong.

"Get out of my face, Emma," I say. I can hear my voice trembling and I know I'm not very scary. She glares at me and steps even closer.

"What are you going to do about it?" Her breath is hot and smells like Nacho Doritos.

I think about how strong Dad is. I don't want to disappoint him. I want him to know that I'm strong too. And maybe if I can hurt Emma this once, she'll leave me alone.

"That's right. Nothing. You can't do anything to me," She says, laughing. She pushes me into the couch.

I stand up and take a deep breath. And then I punch her in the face.

Her eyes are wide, and I know she wasn't expecting me to hit her. My hand feels like it was run over by a car and my legs are shaking but I feel kind of excited. Emma's eyes narrow and fear trickles down my spine. She lunges at me.

She grabs my face and throws me onto the floor. I don't know what to do. I try to crawl away. She kicks me in the stomach. I can't breathe. She pulls my hair and my neck feels like it's going to snap. I scream. She sits on top of me and I know I'm going to die. She's so fat she'll squish me until I explode. Twisting around I bite her arm.

She rolls off me and I try to run away but she grabs my hair. Before I can get free she picks me up and throws me into Dad's wardrobe. My leg feels like it's on fire and I can't move.

"If you ever hit me again, I'll kill you." Emma says quietly. She spits in my face before going up to our room with the bag of chips.

I put my head down on the carpet and cry until I hear Dad on the deck outside. I don't want him to see me like this. He'll know I lost another fight. I stand up and limp towards the bathroom.

"Teester, Emma? I'm home and I brought dinner." He sounds happy. He must have had a good time at work. I don't want to tell him about what happened. I'll ruin his day.

"I'm about to take a bath." I try to close the door.

"Before you get in the tub, I need to pee. My sugar has been high all day."

"Chocolate?" I ask, knowing that he would risk taking extra shots of insulin and being yelled at by his diabetes specialist for anything chocolate coated.

"Yeah, half a donut this morning," he smiles, sheepishly.

I step to the side of the door. "You know that's not good for you, right?"

"Yes, Doctor Tara. I'll try to be better." He brushes past me and I gasp. My leg feels like someone just kicked it.

"What's wrong?"

"Nothing," I lie. I pull on some of my long hair and try to smile.

"What happened?"

I drop my hands to my side. I know it's too late to lie about what happened. He's like a human lie detector test. I sigh and say, "I lost another fight."

"You hit her back?"

"I punched her first."

"Good job," he laughs, "That's my girl."

"But I still lost. She threw me into your wardrobe." I stare at my feet and wiggle my toes. I hate how Emma always wins. I don't know why she was so upset about the chips. I wonder if there is something more that she is mad about. Maybe it's because of her real dad wanting nothing to do with her and my dad actually sticking around. I wonder if it is about how I am so different than her too.

"Let me see." Dad points to my leg.

I wince as I peel off my pants. A black bruise covers my entire left thigh. I've never seen a bruise that dark before. "That must be where the corner of the wardrobe hit," I say.

"Lift your shirt. I want to check your back."

"Why?"

"I want to make sure your spine didn't hit it too."

I pull my shirt up. "What's there?" I ask.

"A bruise on your ribs that's the size of my hand. How'd you get that?"

"She kicked me a few times." I say.

"At least it's not your spine. I'm going to put you into some sort of fighting class."

Before I can say anything, he turns around and walks towards the stairs. Before the yelling starts I lock the bathroom door and sink into the bath.

Dad still isn't home and probably won't be for a few more hours. It's his first parent teacher night as a teacher and he wants to stay late to make sure he talks with everyone. Hopefully it goes by fast. I turn on the TV to National Geographic.

I've been waiting all week for the show about Egypt. The introduction music starts and sounds so exotic. I have never heard the sound before. A shot of the pyramids fill the screen and I wonder what it would have been like to be there when they were being built.

"Get out of our way," Mom says.

I get off the couch and sit on the floor quickly, so I don't miss a thing. Mom sits on the couch with Emma and turns the channel. Instead of watching pyramids and mummies and cursed tombs, Jerry Springer fills the TV. I hate this show. I stand up and go to the table for my book.

"While you're up, get me a candy bar from the freezer," Emma says.

"No."

"Just do it, Tara." Mom rolls her eyes and turns the TV up.

"I don't know why she can't get up off her fat butt and get it herself," I mumble.

Emma turns and glares at me. "Excuse me?"

"You heard me." I turn to walk up the stairs to our room. Irritation fills me at the thought of missing my Egyptian show in order to watch idiots fight on stage. Before I can make it up three steps, I hear the couch creak. I turn back to look into the living room and see Emma leaning towards me.

"Don't ever call me fat, you little bitch." Emma hisses at me.

"If you take up half the couch all for yourself without having your legs up than you're fat."

She lunges off the couch and tries to hit me. I dodge and smile at her.

"Just because you're in some fighting class doesn't mean you're better than me," Emma yells. She punches my left arm and I swing with my right. My fist hits her ear and makes a popping sound. She bellows like a hippo and I kick her in the leg before I back away slowly.

"Come on Emma, hit her," Mom says from the couch.

Emma kicks at me but I block it like Sensei taught me. I think I'm going to win this one. Dad will be so proud, and Emma will finally leave me alone. I punch her in the stomach and back away before she can hit me.

"You're so cocky. Just like your Dad." Mom glares at me and motions for Emma to hit me again.

I step to the side as Emma punches again. I'm not fast enough to get away though and she hits my shoulder. I stumble into the staircase. I turn around, ready to kick, but Mom stands up and walks over to us. I sit on the stairs so that I can catch my breath. I bet Mom is going to yell at us for fighting again. I'll probably be grounded and Emma will just go back to watching her show.

Mom looks down at me and grabs my hands. "Come on Emma, get her."

I don't know what to do. Emma grins at me as she walks over.

"Try to get away now, Tara," Emma laughs. She slaps my face. Hard. Then she looks at Mom.

"I didn't say to stop," Mom says.

"Mom, let me go!" I yell.

I try to squirm away, but Mom pushes me down until I'm lying on the stairs. I'm pinned. The edge of a stair digs into my back as Emma punches me. They're both laughing. It's hot and hard to breathe. I can't remember any of my training. I scream.

"Shut up," Mom says, "You deserve this."

"Yeah, you stupid brat." Emma slaps me again.

I don't think they will stop. They're just going to keep going. I think about how disappointed Dad will be each time

Emma punches me. I think about how strong and brave he is. No one would even try to fight him. And even if they did, he would know what to do. I wish I was more like him.

Emma laughs and spit falls onto me. She punches my nose. I can feel the blood running down my face. My eyes fill with tears and I try to keep them from falling.

"Oh, now you're going to cry? Little *Princess* can't handle it, but she likes to talk tough," Emma says as she grabs my shoulders. "You going to cry? Poor little baby." She lifts my shoulders up and slams me down into the stairs.

I know I have to do something, or I'll probably die. I take a breath and relax. I hold it and go limp.

"Come on and cry, Tara. Daddy's little fighter is going to cry," Mom says and laughs with Emma. She looks back at me. "Hold on Emma," she says, "She's not breathing." She lets go of me and pulls Emma off.

I know what to do.

Take a deep breath. Knee up. Toes pointed. Snap it quick. Kick hard.

My foot hits Emma in the face and her head snaps back. She lands on the floor. I kick Mom in the stomach with my other foot and she falls on top of Emma. I crawl over them and run.

The front door is open and I'm down the cement stairs before I hear them coming for me. I get onto the highway that we live on and keep running. With each step I say "Don't cry. Don't cry. Don't cry."

Firsts

I speed walk the entire quarter mile from the bus stop to my house. The two-lane road is busy, and I try to stay in the soft dirt on the edge to be safe. I don't notice the run-down houses or the barking dogs. I just think about how I have to practice my clarinet.

The small black case hangs at my side as I climb the 13 stairs up to my deck. My first performance for Rim of the World High School's Marching Band is this weekend and I'm terrified. I can't read music as well as the other students because, unlike them, I did not start playing clarinet in the fifth grade because we couldn't afford the instrument. Instead, I was able to have my sister's old clarinet in seventh grade. The extra years the other students had to learn how to read music really shows if you compare our sheets of music. Their sheets are generally free from writing while mine is covered in tiny letters to tell me which note to play and sometimes even little pictures of which keys to press. I know that I shouldn't rely on writing in the notes, but I'll worry about reading music after this weekend.

Now that I'm in high school, I can be in the marching band. We practice after school on Tuesdays, but I'm still not confident with myself. We must have all four songs memorized and march in a parade this weekend and every time I think about it I feel queasy. I want to be as good as the rest of the players so that I can fit in.

Being a freshman means that I only get the backup parts in the songs, but if I can prove to Mr. Jefferson, the director, that I can play well I will be able to join Wind Ensemble.

Wind ensemble is full of the best players in band and they get to play more difficult and exciting music. They even get their own performances and field trips. I want to prove to Dad that the money he had to spend on my uniform and fixing the clarinet will be worth it.

Emma used to be in band, but when she dropped out of high school she decided that band was just as lame as algebra and composition. She likes to make fun of me for being a band geek and Mom always joins in. I want to prove to Mom and Emma that I'm good enough to be in wind ensemble- something Emma never managed to do. Maybe then they'll think I'm cool. I never realized at the time that if I achieved something that Emma had wanted but had never been able to get that it would just make her jealous and ostracize me more. At fourteen I just want to make them proud. Proud enough to stop teasing me and maybe even let me into their world just a little bit. Because even after all the abuse, I just want to feel like I belong.

As I open the front door I'm surprised to find Dad reaching for his keys. He's wearing old jeans with holes and stains in them and a ratty old shirt.

"Why're you home from work already?" I ask as I set my clarinet case on the table. I kick off my shoes and head to the kitchen for a snack.

"It was a half day. I'm actually going to go to urgent care."

I watch him while my frozen burrito heats up in the microwave. He is pale and a little sweaty.

"You think it's just a cold?" I take the burrito out and take a bite. The steam burns my tongue and I grab a glass of water. The chilly water feels good and I drink two glasses before finishing my burrito.

"I hope so. I'll be gone for a few hours. What're you going to do today?" He ties his tennis shoes and slips his insulin case into his backpack.

"I have to practice my music for the parade."

"You'll do great. I wish I could come see you guys march but Escondido is too far for me to drive this weekend."

"It's nice that you want to come, though." I rinse my mouth out with some water to make sure that no food chunks will get into my clarinet.

Dad smiles and kisses me on the forehead. "Just try to stay in the laundry room so Mom and Emma leave you alone."

"Ok, drive safe."

After he leaves, I take my case and a chair into the laundry room. The tile is cold, and the washer is loud, but it's a good place to practice because the ceilings are high and let the sound reverberate.

I unlatch the case. The shiny black instrument lays in five pieces. I pull the two longest ones out and try to fit them together. But the corks in-between the pieces are new and make it difficult to slide the sections into each other. I grab what looks like a Chap Stick container out of my case and open it. The yellow cork grease is used to help lubricate the pieces so that it will be easy to take the instrument apart and put it back together. I rub the grease onto each cork until there is a thick layer. When I push the pieces together it makes a sucking sound, but it slides in smoothly.

I quickly put the rest of the instrument together and take a minute to admire it. The shiny metal keys contrast nicely with the black body. The instrument is almost two feet long, thin, and has a pretty tone when played. I pull out the 2.5 wooden reed and stick it in my mouth. This little thing is what makes all the sound. It's connected to the mouthpiece and when I blow against it, it vibrates. Those vibrations are what makes the sound depending on what keys I press down.

I fiddle with my music while I wait for the reed to get wet. The Christmas songs that we are playing are not too difficult but each time we play them from memory I forget certain sections and then I mess up and play the wrong notes. I don't want to do that during the parade because it will cost the band points. The parade is the first judged competition for our marching band this year. We will be judged on how clean and similar our uniforms are, on the music, and on how well we march as a group.

I take a deep breath and try to relax. As long as I practice for the next five hours, I should be fine. I attach the wooden reed to the mouthpiece and tighten the metal ligature that holds it in place. I run my fingers over the familiar keys and take a deep breath. I close my eyes and play a few scales. As my clarinet warms up, and my fingers, I play faster until the scales all run into each other like one continuous song.

Finally, I open my eyes and play through the parade music. I play through the songs again and again until my fingers hurt and my lips feel like they're going to fall off. I pull my clarinet apart into two main sections and lay them on top of a towel on my chair. I stretch my fingers and walk into the kitchen.

"Are you finally done?" Mom yells from the living room. She is sitting on the couch watching TV. I didn't notice her come down from her room.

"No, I've got to practice some more without the music to see if I have it memorized." I drink a few glasses of water and try to ignore the whispers from the couch.

"Well go outside then. I don't want to hear you anymore."

I don't want to argue so I take my music and clarinet outside. I stand on my music, so it doesn't blow away, and close my eyes. Hopefully I will remember all the notes.

The December air is chilly and after running through the music a few times my fingers are numb and it's hard to play. I stay outside for another half an hour, but when the sun sets I grab my music and go back inside.

My glasses fog up because it's nice and warm inside and I wait for them to clear. The TV is blaring and I hope that it will drown out my sound. I made the same mistakes over and over outside so I know exactly which section of the song I have to work on memorizing. I think if I run through the section a few times tonight and then practice tomorrow in class I should be fine.

I take a deep breath, raise my mouthpiece and blow. The beginning on a jazzy jingle bells floats out of the bell on my clarinet and I hit every note just when I am supposed to. I feel good until I hear someone walking into the kitchen. I try to ignore them but I'm too distracted and I hit the wrong key. A horribly high-pitched squeak fills the laundry room.

I face the door and Mom is staring at me.

"I thought I told you to go outside. I don't want to hear your... *music* anymore."

I can feel my ears growing hot with embarrassment and I try to act like I'm not upset. "It's too cold and dark outside to practice. I just need to run through it a few more times."

"Put it away. You're giving me a headache." She pulls a bag of chips out of the cupboard and heads back into the living room.

"Mom, I have to practice a few more times. I have to have this memorized by Saturday!" I follow her into the living room. I know my voice is a little higher than normal because I'm stressed out. I *need* to practice a few more times tonight.

"Stop squeaking at me and go away."

"But I can't practice in my room because Emma is in there and won't let me," I yell. "I *have* to get this section down or I could cost the whole band points."

"I don't care. Put it away and do something else." Mom's face is getting red and I know she's mad.

"I can't. I'll just be quiet. It will only take a few minutes." I turn to go back into the laundry room, but she takes my shoulder and pushes me towards the stairs instead.

"Put it away!" She yells, "I don't know why that is so god-damn hard for you to understand."

"I can't! I have to practice." I yell back. I know that yelling is probably not the best idea, but I'm stressed out about the performance and if I can't practice I will not be able to prove to anyone that I'm good enough to deserve the instrument.

"Put the fucking thing away before I throw it away." She takes a step closer to me until her face is in mine.

"I have to finish! I have to have it all memorized by Saturday! I just have class tomorrow and then Saturday morning we leave early and won't have time to practice."

"I don't care."

She reaches for my clarinet and I'm not fast enough to keep it from her. She clutches the top half and pulls. Hard. As if in slow motion I see the clarinet start to slide apart. The mustard colored cork grease squishes as the clarinet flies into two pieces. The end of Mom's half hits her in the forehead and she stumbles.

Before I can say anything, Mom throws the top half she is holding into the fireplace. The small mouthpiece shatters against the bricks and the wooden reed splits almost in half and falls out of the ligature. The rest of the body bounces a few times before rolling onto the delicate keys.

My heart stops. I stand perfectly still, looking at my broken clarinet.

"How could you? Band is the only thing that I have at school. My only friends are in band!" I scream. I've never yelled at her like this before. "I need that for this weekend and you just *broke* it!" Anger bubbles up inside of me and I walk towards her. "How could you destroy the only thing I'm good at!" I get close to her and am surprised to see that she looks scared. I shove her shoulders and she stumbles backwards again. My hands shake and I think about hitting her. I want to hit her. I think about all the crap she has done but nothing is as worse as breaking my instrument.

"You hit me in the head with it you little bitch!"

"You hit yourself in the head, you idiot! The instrument comes apart if you pull it. How can you be so dumb!" My throat hurts from yelling so loud but I don't care. Nothing matters now that my clarinet is broken. I know we don't have enough money to fix it and that I will probably have to quit band.

"Don't you dare call me names. Get out of my face before you regret it, crybaby."

Tears stream down my face. But instead of being from sadness, they are caused by rage. I feel like my whole body is shaking. I didn't know that it was because of all the adrenaline at the time, but it didn't matter. "I regret being related to you, moron!"

Mom digs her nails into my upper arm and shoves me across the living room. "Go to your fucking room before I beat your ass."

Her face is red, and I know she is not joking. I pick up my clarinet but leave the shards that used to be my mouthpiece, and run up to my room. Thankfully Emma is not in here and I crawl up into the top bunk and sob into my pillow.

Band is the only thing that is just mine. I have to share everything else with Emma and Finn and we are too poor to pay for me to be in soccer or dance like I want. Band is the one thing that I can do after school to make friends and play music. Playing music is something special. I become someone else who matters and has a specific part. If that part isn't played, the entire band of 200 people could fail; the song becoming meaningless.

I think about all my new friends. For the first time, ever, I have friends that aren't my cat or little brother. There are nearly 200 people that I get to spend time with. Some I know just in passing like John who looks like he should be in football more than band with how muscular he already is. But then there are others who I'm close with. Hana plays clarinet and takes extra time each day to teach me what her private instructor has taught her. She helps me read the music and we even have a few other classes together. She sits next to me in honors English and we sometimes eat lunch together. Then there's Ben who also plays clarinet and he is funny and weird. He's always building robots and batteries from potatoes. There are even older students like Jessica, a junior, who asks me for advice. Her boyfriend is a jerk a lot of the time and she likes to complain about him to me.

I cry even harder into my pillow as I realize that my only friends will forget about me once I'm not in band anymore. They will be busy practicing marching together and learning new songs that I will never know.

I cry until I don't have any tears left, my anger leaving with them. I sit up and look at my clarinet. The section that mom threw seems ok. One of the silver keys is a little bent, but it still moves the right way. Hopefully it's not broken. Maybe, if I get a job after school, I can save up enough to fix the mouthpiece.

As I turn it over in my hands, I hear something coming up the stairs. I locked the door after I came in so Mom couldn't come bother me anymore. She will probably just go into her room and watch a movie.

There is a loud tapping on the door before a deep voice says, "Open this door, now."

It's not Dad's voice and no other man should be here. I don't know who it is but I don't want to open the door.

"This is the Sheriff's department. If you don't open the door now, I will break it open." His voice is deep and loud, and he sounds deadly serious.

I scramble off my bed and open the door. A man with no hair fills the tiny doorway. His tan shirt is pressed and gleams in the dim light. He has big black boots on and I can't help but notice a full duty belt complete with a taser and hand gun.

"Is your name Tara?"

I nod.

"I need you to come downstairs. Walk in front of me and don't try to run."

I don't know why I would want to run from him, but I just nod and do as he says. I try to take a deep breath but can only manage shallow ones. I feel lightheaded as I walk into the living room with the Sheriff close behind me. Mom is standing near the front door with an ice pack on her forehead and Emma is smiling on the couch.

"Sit on the chair. I have some questions for you." The Sheriff pulls out a notepad and paper while I sit. I tap my feet on the carpet and try not to show how scared I am.

"Do you have a clarinet?" He glares at me.

"Yes, it's upstairs."

"What were you doing with it tonight?"

"I was playing some Christmas songs for a parade on Saturday."

"Your mother tells me that she asked you to pack up for the night and you called her names. Is that true?"

"We got in a fight because I wanted to finish practicing the music and it was too cold to play outside anymore."

"After that, you hit your mother in the head with your instrument, is that correct?"

"No!" I try to stay calm but my heart is pounding. Why would Mom say I hit her? I know that I wanted to hit her, but that was after she broke my mouthpiece. I look at Emma's smug face and know that she probably had something to do with Mom calling the cops on me.

"So, your mother and sister are both lying to me?" I can tell from his voice that he doesn't believe me.

"Mom tried to pull my clarinet out of my hands but I just put cork grease on and it came apart and she hit herself with it."

"You're trying to tell me that she hit herself in the head and then called the cops on you? Why would she do that?"

"I don't know." I look at mom and she just glares at me. I look up into the Sheriff's face. I've never felt this betrayed before. "I yelled at her and called her names and pushed her after she broke my clarinet. But I swear I never hit her with it. I can show you how it comes apart if you want."

"Go get it and come back immediately."

I rush up the stairs and catch Emma laughing behind the Sheriff's back. I find my clarinet in my blankets and try to steady my hands. I walk down the stairs and show it to him.

"These pieces go together to make the whole thing." I put the two sections together and hand it to him. "I put cork grease inside to make it easier to put together. When Mom pulled on it, it just came apart."

He tugs on it softly and the two sections slide apart.

"Then it hit her and she got mad and threw it into the fireplace. The mouthpiece broke." I point to the debris that are still lying on the red bricks. "That's when I got mad and shoved her. I also called her names." There's no point in lying to him about what I did. Hopefully, he can tell that I'm being truthful about everything.

The officer scribbles a few things into his notebook before turning to Mom.

"Do you need a medic to come look at that for you?" His voice sounds sarcastic even though his face is serious. I hope that means he believes me.

Mom takes a deep breath and shakes her head. "I don't think so. As long as I just take it easy and keep ice on it I think it will be ok." Her voice is soft and airy and I can tell that she is acting like she is in more pain that she actually is.

"Would you like to press charges for assault?" he taps his pen on the edge of his notebook. His voice is still sarcastic so it takes me a minute to understand what he said. Assault! Something like that could go on my record. I might even have to go to jail. Panic fills me until I feel like I'm going to fall off the chair.

"Assault? But I didn't do anything." I try to keep my voice calm, but I hear it and it is loud and high pitched.

"Please let your mother answer." He looks at me and for just a second his face seems to soften.

"Mom, you know I didn't hit you. Come on, are you really going to send me to juvenile hall?" I can't imagine what being in juvenile hall is like. I don't know what I'm going to do if he takes me there.

"I think she learned her lesson for tonight, officer." Mom says.

The officer turns to me and takes a deep breath. "I want you to go upstairs and stay there the rest of the night. This is my card. If you need me for any reason, call me. Now go on." He hands me the card and motions for me to go upstairs. I look up into his face and he gives me a tiny wink that only I can see. I hide my happiness as I run up the stairs. I know he must believe me. Before I close my bedroom door I listen to what they're saying.

"Sometimes she just won't listen and goes crazy. Her father thinks she is a perfect angle, but it's times like this that I worry about her," Mom says. Her voice is full of fake concern and I hate how she is lying about me.

"I don't appreciate being called here on false pretenses. There was no attack with a weapon. Wasting my time is a crime and so is filing a false police report. You and your daughter here could be fined or serve time, do you understand?" His voice is deep.

"We didn't lie. Tara's crazy and hit my mom." Emma says.

"If I were you, young lady, I would be quite."

"I wasn't trying to waste your time." Mom sounds a little nervous and I like it. I hope she is just as scared that she's going to jail as I was when the Sheriff first pounded on my door.

"Well you did. If I have to come back here tonight because of something stupid someone is going to go to jail, got it?"

I don't hear an answer before his boots boom through the living room and onto the deck. I close and lock my door.

I can't believe Mom would call the cops and lie about what happened. I know that we fight a lot, but I never expected her to go so far as to almost get me charged with assault. As I lie in bed and wait for Dad to come home I decide that I can never trust Mom again.

I don't know how long I stay in the same position, but eventually I'm sore and need to stretch. I crawl down from my bunk bed and I hear the front door open. I hold my breath and stay still until I hear Dad's voice.

"Tara, come down here." He sounds angry and I wonder what lies Mom and Emma told him. I'm not too worried about it though. He can always tell when I lie so I know he will believe me when I tell him what happened. I run down the stairs and hug him. He's a little sweaty and smells like McDonalds, but I don't care. He's strong and I know he won't let anything happen to me.

"What happened while I was gone?"

I stand up straight and say, "Mom and I got in a fight because she didn't want me to practice. She grabbed my clarinet and it came apart and hit her in the head so she threw it into the fireplace and called the cops on me. A Sheriff came and almost took me away for assaulting her."

Dad whole body gets still and I look at his face. He looks at Mom who is sitting on the couch and I have never seen him this angry before.

"What the fuck is wrong with you? How could you call the cops on your own daughter? Why do you hate her so much?" His voice is quiet and raspy from being sick, but I think it's scarier this way then when he yells.

"She hit me in the head. What was I supposed to do?" Mom yells.

"You hit yourself in the head, you fucking moron. Don't ever call the cops on her again and blame her for your stupidity. You're lucky they didn't take her to juvie."

"Are you going to threaten me now?" Mom stands up walks over to us. She pokes dad in the chest and stands so close to him that it looks like they might kiss.

"Yeah, I am," He pokes her in the chest so hard that she takes a step back. "If you ever do something like that again I will divorce your ass and take the kids. I can't believe you can treat your own flesh and blood this way. You have serious mental problems."

"I wouldn't treat her like this if she didn't act like a selfish little brat all the time. Just like you." She turns and glares at me. "She gets her way all the time and is a little bitch to me and Emma every day. But she's your *Prinzessin* so I can't discipline her."

"Calling the cops and threating to take her away isn't discipline. It's bullying. You've hated her since she was born, Natalie, cut the crap. I've had to step up and do everything for her while you're off taking your daughter everywhere she wants to go," He points to Emma on the couch and then to me, "Newsflash, you have two daughters. Start acting like a mom to both of them."

"I'm not going to take this bullshit. Come on Emma, let's go."

She slams the door on her way out and I hear her car speed off into the night. I turn to look at dad and reach for him. He pulls me into a side hug and scratches my back.

"I'm so sorry dad. I didn't mean for us to fight. I just really needed to practice and then when she threw my clarinet I was so mad. I yelled at her and shoved her."

"Good. It's time she realized she can't bully you around with Emma. I don't know what her problem is with you, but she has to get over it."

"I'm sorry I always cause problems." My chest is heavy with guilt. I hate being the reason Dad fights with Mom. I feel like all I ever do is fight with Mom and Emma and that causes Dad to fight with them too. I feel like I am tearing up my family.

"It's not your fault. Your mom is the one who causes the problems. If she just realized that you are just as much her daughter as Emma is, then everything would be fine. She must have some guilt complex with Emma. Maybe she feels bad that she didn't stay with Emma's dad or something."

"Has she really always had problems with me? Even when I was a baby?"

"Yeah, she never really took care of you. I always did the bottles and the diaper changes. Except the poopy ones, I would just hose you off or stick you in the shower." He laughs and I know he's picturing it. "But you always slept with me at night, even as a newborn, while she was upstairs with Emma."

I sit down on the couch and think about when Finn was born and how tiny and cute he was. I could never have hated him or been mean to him. How can anyone dislike a baby, let alone their own? The familiar self-conscious feelings start to come to the surface. There must be something wrong with me. Maybe I cried too much when I was little, or maybe I'm just too annoying. I must have done something to make Mom so upset with me. I take a deep breath and try to push away the feelings of self-loathing. I'm getting straight A's so far and I've been making friends. I know that I have good qualities and I try to prove them to everyone, but it doesn't help these feelings go away.

"What time do you have to be at the high school on Saturday for your parade?"

It takes me a minute to process his words. I shake my head and say, "I'm not going. I don't have a mouthpiece."

"I'm going to take the day off tomorrow because I'm still feeling sick. I'll take you down to the music store in the morning and we'll get you a new mouthpiece. Then I'll drop you off at the high school in time to practice since it's your last day in class before the parade."

"But it's too expensive."

"I don't care how expensive it is. We're getting you one." He smiles and plops down onto the couch next to me. I sigh and hand Dad the remote, feeling guilty about the extra expense. I know that there's no point in arguing with him about how much money he has already spent on my clarinet. When he makes up his mind, nothing is going to change it.

Nothing helps me to forget about my problems like watching the history channel with Dad. He turns on the World War II series we have been watching and we sink into the cushions together. Preferring to watch the horrors of war over talking about our own.

30 Weeks

I finish rubbing my body butter onto my belly and feel so relieved that the itchy feeling goes away. My doctor said that being itchy when pregnant is normal, but he didn't say how intense it could be. I guess it's just from having to stretch out my skin to accommodate the growing babies.

Alex helps me put my shoes on and we pile into the car. He drives slowly as I pull out my notebook and study for the last final that I will take on campus. Even though I won't have to come down to campus next quarter, I will still be taking classes. I only need three more to graduate with my BA in English and I don't want to put it off. Hopefully the twins won't be born until after I'm done.

"So I have been thinking about the name 'Aurora' a lot." Alex looks at me, and smiles.

"I haven't heard of that one before," I say, glancing through my physics notes.

"I made it from the letters of our names."

"It's pretty. But it will have to sound good with the other name we pick to. And it can't rhyme. I don't want names that rhyme." I put my notes away and pull my water bottle out of my bag. I take a drink of my peppermint water, hoping the nausea will go away.

"Well I really wanted to name them Karly and Charlie!"
He laughs.

"No way."

"Kara and Sarah?"

"No." I laugh at him and we keep finding rhyming names
until we get to campus.

He pulls up as close as he can get to the biology building
and parks on the side walk.

"What about 'Lillian'?" He asks, pulling my bag out for me
and helping me stand up. I never thought I would have problems getting out of the car before, but because my stomach is
bigger than a basketball my balance is off.

"That's a nice one. But does it go with Aurora?"

"Happy Birthday to Aurora and Lillian, Happy birthday
to you," Alex sings, "It sounds good to me."

I laugh at him and give him a kiss before grabbing my bag.
"I'll think about it."

"Do you want me to carry your bag in for you?"

I look at the building and how close it is. It will only take
me a few minutes to get there. I have been so sick lately that I
don't have any energy to do anything, but taking a small walk
will be good for me, the babies, and my bag isn't too heavy.
"No, I'll be fine. Go to your own final!"

He kisses me and jumps into the driver's seat. Before
he leaves he waves. I walk down the cobble stone walkway
and enjoy the warm breeze. The walkway starts to incline
slightly and before I know it I'm out of breath. I set my bag
down near a tree and think about the names Aurora and
Lillian. They are so different from each other but I like that.
I wonder if the girls will be really different or be more in
sync with each other. I put my hands over my belly and sing
happy birthday to them using the possible names. When I

finish they both start to kick and I feel like I'm going to pee my pants.

"So I guess we know what your names are, huh?" I whisper to them.

"Can I help you with your bag?" a young security guard holds out is hand and smiles at me.

"That would be great." I smile back and hand it to him. He carries it carefully and walks with me to class.

"So how far along are you?"

"30 weeks with twins."

I expect his surprised face and laugh when he looks at my stomach.

"There are really two of them in there?"

"Yeah. It's weird and pretty awesome at the same time."

"You're like a little group all on your own!" He smiles.

I smile back at him and think about how good that makes me feel. I like finally being part of a group, knowing that we are together and knowing that we all will need each other.

"Are you graduating soon?" He opens the door to the biology building for me.

"Yeah, next quarter."

"Well if you need any help getting to class or anything you can call this number and someone can drive you in the little go-carts." He hands me his card and points to the right number.

"Thank you so much! I might need that when I get even bigger." I laugh. I can't imagine being bigger than I already am now. I know it will happen though because I still have 10 weeks left. My doctor said that the longer the girls stay inside, the better chances they have not needing interventions when they are born.

He hands me my bag and pauses. "Do you have names picked out yet?"

I put my hand on my belly and can feel a little baby underneath the skin moving. "Aurora and Lillian."

"Those are good names." He opens the door and leaves before I can thank him. I wait for a second before going into the room. I want to enjoy the moment with my little girls. Just the three of us.

Worn

With one minute until I have to leave, I frantically throw clothes out of the laundry basket, looking for my favorite shirt. It's black with small red roses sprinkled on it and its tight fitting which makes it perfect to wear under my marching band uniform.

"Tara, let's go!" Dad yells from the front deck.

I look in the dirty clothes hamper too, but don't have any luck. My shirt must be in the washer. I abandon the search grabbing the first shirt out of the dryer and run out of the door. I jump down the 13 cement stairs and climb into Dad's car.

I fiddle with my clarinet case's handle as I wait for Dad to finish checking on his new cherry tree. I'm nervous and excited all at once. Today is my first competition for my high school marching band. I run through a list of the things that I need and my heart nearly stops. I yank open my case to double check that my new mouthpiece is there and smile when I see it nestled into the soft pads.

Yesterday, Dad brought me down to the music store and got me a shiny new mouthpiece along with some new cork grease and a Disneyland Goofy sticker for my case. It was so much fun. He even listened to me practice my music last night. I know he's trying to make up for how Mom broke my clarinet yesterday and when I think about it I'm still furious. Mom doesn't seem to understand how badly she hurt me. No matter how many times I explain how her actions hurt me, she never really gets it and always tries to just shrug it off.

A few hours after she broke my clarinet she wanted to watch a movie as a family and when I didn't come down stairs she came up and tried to convince me. She said that family time was important, and I know that, but I was too angry to even sit in the same room with her. My heart races just remembering it. Instead of thinking about it, I bury it deep within myself and focus on today. I can't have any distractions.

"You ready? You have everything you need, right?" Dad gets into the driver's seat of our Kia and turns the car on. The oldies station fills the car and he hums along.

"I think so. I know all the songs and I have the ten bucks for lunch."

"Your uniform is already at school?"

"Yeah, we don't change into them until right before we march in the parade."

He nods and pulls into the McDonalds drive thru. He orders us each a breakfast sandwich and hash brown and he gets me a large orange juice.

"Dad, you don't have to buy me breakfast." I worry about how expensive it is. I know that he is a teacher at a middle school in San Bernardino now and we aren't too tight with money anymore, but I still worry about having enough. I don't like to remember when we couldn't buy a lot of groceries or when we had to cancel the internet and TV. I know he is still trying to make up for what happened with Mom. My anger flares up and I hate how he feels guilty for something she did. He is always taking responsibility for her problems and I don't understand why. Maybe it has something to do with her helping him get over his first wife and the horrible divorce he went through. And maybe it's because I know, deep down, that he loves her and hopes that she will become the woman he fell in love with again.

"Teester, it's just a few dollars. Don't worry so much." He hands me the food and pulls back into the road.

The drive only takes fifteen minutes and I'm still working on my orange juice when Dad pulls into the high school's parking lot. There are two yellow school busses parked in front with a big crowd of students. It almost looks like a beehive with all the people moving around the sign in table.

Dad pulls up to the very front and puts the car into park. I'm a little embarrassed that we are right next to the busses because people are looking at me, but when Dad gives me a kiss on the forehead, I forget about them. He always makes me feel calm.

"You're going to do great, Teester. Ich liebe dich."

"Love you too, Dad." I smile and jump down from the car and wave while he drives away. There are so many people around me all pushing, shoving and yelling that I feel like I'm in an ocean of people. I look down at my shirt and realize that it is one of Finn's t-shirts and has a giant blue T-Rex across the front. I can't believe that I'm in a little boy's shirt around the entire band. There are people in every grade and I was really hoping to make a good impression on some of them so that they could help me with the music for the next performance. I take a deep breath and try to pretend like I choose this shirt as I fight my way to the front steps and yell my last name to the band booster. She makes a mark on a sheet of paper and motions for me to move along.

I spot long black hair in the crowd and head for it.

"Nice shirt." John says and pushes me a bit.

"Shut up." I say, pushing him back.

"No, I was being serious. It has a cool contrast of colors." He smiles.

"It's my little brothers. I grabbed it on accident. Don't tell anyone."

"Your secret is safe with me. Who are you going to sit with on the bus?" He asks.

"I'm trying to find Hana. I thought I saw her hair but now it's gone." I scan the crowd where I thought she had been, but she must have moved on.

He points behind me. I turn and smile as Hana waves me over. She is way taller than me and when she pulls me into a hug my head rests just under her chin. She puts her chin on top of my head and rubs it into my hair, laughing. "You're so tiny and cute. I just love you!" She says, squeezing me some more.

"Not all of us can have mile long legs, Hana." I squeeze her back.

"Hana, let her go. You can't keep her. She's all mine" Haru, Hana's older brother, shoves her a little and pulls me from her arms. He gives me a quick hug and winks at me before going to the front of the bus with his older friends.

"You want to sit with us? I promised Lei I'd sit with her, but there will be enough room for you since you're so small," Hana jokes as she rests her arms onto my shoulders.

"Sure." I smile. Lei joins us but pulls out some makeup and drags her eyeliner across the top of her eye. She makes it thick and leaves a long pointed line at the crease, which accentuates her already pointed eyes.

"You want me to do yours?" Lei asks, "I won't give you the Asian eyes though. You would look weird with them."

"No, I'm good. Thanks." I say and smile as Hana rolls her eyes. She always makes fun of Lei for drawing attention to her Asian background. Hana tries to blend in, even though being half Japanese makes it a little difficult in a small school like ours.

We talk about the parade and how there is going to be a carnival afterwards for the awards show. Hana wants to ride the Ferris wheel and get some funnel cakes. She says they are the best, but I've never had them before. I'm too anxious about my stupid shirt and the performance to actually join the conversation but being part of a group is nice.

It takes another half an hour for everyone to check in. Once the director is sure that everyone is here, we all line up to get onto the busses. People push and try to jump to the front to ensure they have good seats. Mr. Jefferson has to yell for everyone to quiet down before he lets us on the bus. The noise dies down a little bit but picks back up in just a few minutes.

"All freshmen in the back!" someone yells. Others laugh and we get shoved to the back of the line.

After slowly making our way to the bus doors we have to wait for Mr. Jefferson to count each of us and mark it down on a sheet of a paper. He does this every time we get on the busses, to make sure we are all accounted for.

Hana and Lei climb up before me and I have to wait while Mr. Jefferson flips his paper over. He gives me a weird look before nodding to me. I know he looked at my shirt and how ridiculous it must look on me. My ears start to get hot and I know I'm blushing with embarrassment. I climb the three small steps up and wait for the kids in the front seat to move their bags out of the way. The bus is loud and a wave of warm air hits my face even though it is six in the morning. I look from side to side to find Hana and Lei sitting together in the third seat from the front. My hands start to sweat as I realize there are no empty seats in front of them.

"Can we all fit in one seat?" I ask them.

"My sax is taking up too much room," Lei says pointing to her huge case that is filling up a section of the seat. She shrugs and untangles her headphones. If she could just put that on the floor there would be room for me, but I know how stubborn she is and how it would be pointless to ask.

"Sorry Tara, try sitting near us though," Hana looks guilty as she looks around at the full bus. I turn to look down the aisle and notice the seat directly behind her only has one person in it.

He has hair that is in between a dark blonde and a light brown and is facing the window. His big case sits on the seat next to him and he's reading a book. I feel a little awkward asking to sit with him, but it's the only spot available.

Before I ask to sit with him, I hug my case, hoping it will hide some of my ugly shirt.

"Is anyone sitting here?" I ask.

He turns and looks at me. He has big blue eyes and I can't help but think he's good looking. I nervously pull on my shirt as he watches me. Why couldn't I be wearing something pretty, or even remotely girly when I meet a cute guy? I look at his shoulder, so I don't have to see his expression.

He simply moves his case to the floor and turns back towards the window with his book. I guess that means I can sit down. I lay my clarinet in between us and wonder why he didn't just tell me to sit down. Maybe he's shy or maybe he's in a really good spot in his book. He looks familiar, but I can't remember his name.

"My name's Tara. What's yours?"

He turns to face me and says, "Alex."

"You're a freshman, too, right?"

He nods.

"What do you play?" I pull my legs up to my chest and smile trying to ignore the awkwardness.

"Trumpet."

"I play clarinet. I've played since seventh grade. What about you?" I know I'm asking a lot of questions, but that's what I do when I feel awkward around someone. Especially someone who's attractive.

"Since fifth grade."

I smile at him, but he turns back to his book. I don't want to stop talking with him though, so I ask, "What classes are you in?"

He puts his book down, with a half-smile on his face, and turns to me. "Just the regular ones I guess."

"Like what?" I hope he thinks I'm nice and will talk with me some more.

"Honors English, geometry, drama, biology, band, and Spanish."

"Do you have Miss Henry for Honors English? I have her second period," I say.

"Yeah, but I have her first."

"Did you like *To Kill a Mockingbird*?" I ask. The book is becoming one of my favorites. I like the idea of having a Boo Radley character in a neighborhood, looking out for children who may be in danger or lonely. I like to pretend that the house across my street belongs to Boo Radley and that one day I will finally meet someone who understand me.

"Yeah. My dad used to teach it, so I used his old book with his notes in it."

"I bet that helped with the essay."

"Yeah, she said I got the highest score out of all her classes." He smiles mischievously.

I shake my head, "Cheater."

"It's not cheating, it's assisted learning," he says with a grin. We both laugh.

"Find your uniform and change," Kali, my section leader, says. She points at the long racks of uniforms next to the three big EZ Up tents.

"Where are the changing rooms?" I look around and notice that the older students are stripping down into their underwear underneath the EZ Ups and putting their uniforms on. All of the freshmen are grouped together in small groups looking wildly out of place. I try to spot Alex, but I can't see him through the crowd. I wonder if we will get to see each other after the parade. I hope we can sit together on the bus again.

"There aren't any, just change here." She pulls off her top. Her bright yellow bra makes her brown skin look even darker in contrast. She doesn't seem shy at all. She pulls off her pants to reveal a matching thong and just stands there for a minute. Several of the boys in our section are staring at her and she doesn't seem to notice. She's too busy rummaging around in her uniform bag.

I look at Hana and she looks shocked that she has to get undressed in public. At least I'm not the only one.

"Damn it, I can't find my shorts. You guys have your bike short on underneath your pants, right?" Kali asks pointing at us.

I nod. At our last rehearsal Mr. Jefferson made it very clear that we needed to wear bike shorts and a tank top underneath our uniforms.

"Well don't just stand around. We warm up in five minutes and you better be dressed by then."

I don't want to be late and get in trouble, so I pull on Hana's hand and drag her towards the EZ Ups. "Let's go find a spot to get dressed, Hana." I try to sound like I'm not stressed out about getting undressed around everyone, but my voice wavers just a little. We find a place near the center of the tent and hang our uniform bags on the metal poles.

"Let's get this over with," I say. I hope that no one is watching me as I unzip my uniform bag and pull out the pants. Maybe if I have them ready, I can just jump right into them without being exposed too long.

I unzip my jeans and pull them off quickly. Even though I'm wearing shorts, they are so tight and tiny that I feel like I'm just in my underwear. I pull on the thick wool pants of the uniform and leave the suspenders down while I pull off my shirt.

I'm wearing a sports bra over my regular bra, like always, but it's still weird to be out in the middle of the day with just my bra on. I try to get my jacket out of the bag, but before I can cover up, I hear a whistle.

I turn and notice a group of older boys watching me and Hana. I can feel my face turn bright red and I look at her. She looks horrified.

I pull my suspenders on and then cover up with the jacket. The guys are probably just teasing us. I look at the tops of my breast and notice the thin white stretch marks. After not having to wear a bra in eighth grade, to needing a D cup by the time I started high school, I expected there to be stretchmarks, but I didn't anticipate them showing up on my thighs and hips as well. Dad says that they are just from maturing so quickly and not to worry about them, but I feel fat and embarrassed. I hear Mom's voice in my head and suddenly I feel ashamed and ugly. I zip up my jacket and hear something from behind me.

I turn around and notice one of the tallest guys in band walking towards us. His head nearly touches the EZ up tent, making him taller than six feet. He's a senior and I've never talked to him before. I don't even know his name.

"You sure your suspenders aren't twisted? You might want to take your jacket back off and check."

The look in his eyes is something I have never seen before. I will come to know that look as lust and understand that he'll do anything to get what he wants. I will see it several times and have nightmare about it years later, but for now I just feel a little uncomfortable under the gaze.

"They feel fine, thanks," I say. As I turn away, Hana pulls on my arm and drags me to where our section has gathered. As I follow her, I think about how I was uncomfortable under the older boy's gaze, but at the same time I was a little excited. Excited that someone noticed me. Maybe Mom was wrong about me. Maybe I am attractive, at least to some people. I think about Alex and hope that he is one of those people.

Our section is standing near the trumpets and while we go over our scales and get in tune with each other I look for Alex. He's standing with his trumpet in his hands and chatting with some other students. He's tall and his hair is being swept up in a light breeze. I feel like I just drank a can of soda and the bubbles are trying to escape.

"Let's start from the top." Kali raises her arms and directs our music.

We play the four songs once through then she dismisses us to rest out mouths for the actual parade. I glance up and notice Alex is looking at me. My ears get hot and I hope that the blush doesn't travel to my face as I smile and motion for him to come over.

He jogs up and says, "Hi." His voice is quiet compared to the rest of the people around us. But I have no trouble hearing him.

"Hi," I say while playing with the keys on my clarinet.

"You nervous?" He asks.

"A little. I'm more excited about the carnival."

"It sounds fun, I guess." He kicks a few pebbles around with his feet.

"I've never had a funnel cake and Hana is going to share one with me," I laugh, nervously, and it sounds strange to me. I wonder if this is flirting and if I'm doing it right.

"That's nice." He glances up at my face and then quickly away again.

"Well maybe we can sit together on the bus ride home?" I ask.

He seems to freeze for a second. I wonder if he even likes me at all. Maybe I just want him to. I kick my shoes in the dust and hope he says yes. I feel like an eternity has passed before he smiles.

"Yeah, I'd like that. I'll see you later." He turns and rejoins his friends. I can't help but to smile. I'm a little nervous about the parade, but more nervous about sitting with Alex on the bus again.

Three sharp whistle blows fill the air and means that we have to line up and get prepared to march. I rush to my place on the edge of the band. My fingers are tingling, and I can feel the sweat dripping from underneath the big bucket hat and feather plume that I'm wearing. I wiggle my toes and try to focus on the person's hat in front of me.

"Atten-Hut," yells our Drum Major. We snap to attention and all scream "RIM" together. It echoes in between the busses and the other bands near us all stop and watch. I'm perfectly still. My breathing is controlled and in tune with the person next to me. We don't move until one long whistle blow signals us to raise our instruments. Together we snap them up in place and again, we freeze. It always surprised me that hundreds of people can be so in tune with one another, but after practicing every day after school I know how much discipline it takes. I know that with a table full of judges watching us, we are even more in tune with each other now than we ever have been before.

Two medium length whistles followed by one long one signals the snare drums to tap and after four beats we all start to move. With each single beat of the snare drum our left feet hit the pavement together and we pass by several long tables of judges. After the drums play their solo, we begin the first song.

At Rim of the World High school the wind is known for being strong and dangerous. Since the high school was built right next to a big cliff, the wind will often tear hats and homework away from students and throw them down the side of the mountain to the rocks hundreds of feet below. As I climb off the bus, I notice Alex is waiting for me. The wind seems to pull me from the bus and push me closer to him. It's so strong that I reach out and grab Alex's arm to steady myself.

"Thanks," I say awkwardly as he helps me walk towards the parking lot. He stands in-between me and the wind and acts like a buffer.

"Yeah, no problem."

"So I guess I'll see you Monday for band?" I fidget with my shirt and wish for the millionth time that I had been able to find my favorite shirt this morning. I feel like such a tom boy in Finn's shirt, and for the first time in my life, I wish I was more girly.

"Yeah, I'll find you during nutrition." He smiles and I smile back.

"Alright, well I'll see you later then." I wave to him as I run to Dad's car in the parking lot.

"Hey Teester, so how was the parade?" Dad asks as I climb into the car. He hands me a bag from the store and inside is a burrito made from the deli. I hold it in my hands and let the warmth seep into my cold fingers.

"Good, we got second place." I smile. I know that I'm more excited about my day with Alex, then the competition but I don't tell Dad this. I don't know why I don't share the information, generally I tell dad everything, but part of me wants to keep the jokes, and laughter and bus ride home with Alex all to myself.

"I knew you guys would do great. How was the carnival?"

I think about how I didn't see Alex during the carnival, but it was still fun. "Hana and I shared a funnel cake that was pretty good, but I didn't want to go on the Ferris wheel because it was too high up."

Dad nods his head and reaches for my hand. "I'm glad you had a good day."

We hold hands on the drive home. Just as we enter our neighborhood, I see Robin, the neighbor from down the street, walking her dog. She is the same age as me, but we don't really know each other. Her older sister is friends with Emma, so I try to stay away from her. I don't like to be involved with Emma's friends. As we drive pass her, I think I see small roses on her shirt, but I laugh at myself a little. There is no way she's wearing my shirt. I'm probably just thinking about how bummed I was about not having it today. Instead of meeting the cute boy with a great top, I had to meet him in the embarrassing dinosaur shirt. But I will just make up for that on Monday by wearing my favorite shirt instead.

Just as Dad pulls into the driveway, Mom pulls in right next to us. Everyone piles out of the cars. While Dad goes to check on his trees, Finn runs over to me.

"How'd you do Teester?" he slurs his words because he is sucking on a big jolly rancher.

"Second place." I high-five him. "Where did you guys go?"

"We gave Robin a big bag of clothes that don't fit you anymore." He runs up the stairs happily.

I look towards my Mom and she seems a little jumpy. I hope she's not high, but when she pushes past me, I can smell what reminds me of burnt plastic and I know that she has done drugs today.

"Did you guys go through my clothes?" I try to keep the anxiety out of my voice, but I can't completely hide it and my voice gets a little squeaky. I'm not really particular about what I wear. Generally, I'm in jeans and a t-shirt, but if Mom went through it while high and angry about yesterday, I know everything I like will be gone.

Mom stops on the stairs and turns to face me. "Don't freak out. I got rid of the stuff that doesn't fit you anymore while I was folding the laundry."

"How do you know what fits me and what doesn't if I'm not here?" I worry about what I have left.

"Just shut up. None of the stuff was cute anyways," Emma says.

They push past me and walk up the stairs together. I try to remain calm, but my heart starts to race thinking about what they got rid of. I run around to the back yard and into the sliding glass door in the back of the house just as Mom opens the front door. I race through the small kitchen, living room, and up the stairs.

Before I even get into my room, I know that my beautiful black shirt with the delicate roses are gone. They are on the neighbor girl's shoulders, and I will never be able to wear it to impress Alex. I see a pile of clothes on my dresser and as I shift through them, I feel hallow.

Every single shirt is either an old one of my sisters, which due to her weight will hang off me, or an old one of my little brothers. Granted, Finn's old shirts will fit pretty well, but I don't want to walk around with trucks, Bob the Builder and Spiderman on my shirts my first year of high school. I dig through the clothes and realize that even some of my best jeans are gone and the ones with holes and stains are left.

I throw the clothes on the floor and feel defeated. I wonder if Mom and Emma gave them away because they were mad at me for getting out of going to juvenile hall yesterday, or if it is something more. Maybe it has to do with the fact that I'm thin and they are not and they don't get to wear the types of clothing that I do. Whatever the reason, I know that I will not be able to impress Alex at school on Monday. I feel a little silly that I want to wear something pretty just for a boy, but there was something special about Alex. Even though I was nervous to be around him, it was fun and exciting, and we were able to talk about things that we both liked. He seemed to understand me a little, and I liked that. I hope he felt the same about me.

I rummage around the floor looking for something to read and take my mind off my empty dresser. I find *Lolita* and open the pages again. I wonder in Lolita felt the same way when Humbert was looking at her that I did when that senior was looking at me today. I push the memory away and escape into someone else's nightmare.

Hello Goodbye

Dad has been gone for two days, and so far, I have been left alone. But today is my fifteenth birthday and I know that I can't avoid everyone anymore. I throw on a pair of pants and cover up an old shirt with a sweater.

"Tara!" Finn's yells at me from downstairs.

I open the door and see him holding a big box out in front of him. I wonder what he got for me.

"What's inside?" I ask as I walk down to meet him.

"You've gotta open it to find out!" He runs through the living room and out of the front door laughing the whole way.

I walk down the rest of the stairs and peek out of the front window. He sees me and runs off the deck and around the house. Instead of following him, I weave my way through the messy living room and into the tiny kitchen.

When my parents bought the house five years ago, it seemed so big. The kitchen was almost double the size of our last one, and this house had 3 bedrooms compared to the one small one we were used to but now I feel cramped in this house, too. But the market had been good and we needed a house in 30 days, so Dad bought this one.

I kneel so that Finn can't see me through the window and creep to the laundry room door that is off the kitchen. I look around the frame and past the piles of dirty laundry to the sliding glass door at the back. Finn is walking backwards facing the front of the house holding the big box awkwardly in his arms.

I try to stay quiet but seeing him walk like that with a big box makes me laugh a little. I jump into the laundry room and fling the door open.

"Gottcha!" I scream and grab Finn.

He tries to squirm. He's ten years old and although he's tall he is so skinny that he can't get away from me.

I tickle his sides until he can't breathe and starts to cry a little before I let him go. "Now give me my present or else!" I glare at him, trying to look menacing, but he just smiles back at me.

"Ok," he pants, "But you have to share it with me."

I hold out my hands and he gives me the box. It looks like it could fit a computer inside of it, but it feels completely empty. I look at Finn and notice that he has a sheepish grin spreading across his face.

I open the top of the box and see a little package of Reese's Pieces chocolates snuggled next to some crunched up toilet paper.

"Thanks Finn."

"I know they're your favorite, so I looked inside the couch and I climbed on top of Dad's big closet to get some change and then I walked to Jonny's Market and bought it!"

I think about how much work he had to put into getting me some candy. For a ten-year-old, walking half a mile to the little market and back not to mention having to find all the change would have taken him all morning.

I peel open the package and hand him the first-round piece of chocolate. He shoves the whole thing in his mouth and talks about how he found the box and 'filled' it with toilet paper to make it feel 'full', even though I knew it was basically empty. As I take my first bite, I notice how great it tastes.

"Oh, and I can't hang out tonight because I'm going over to Carter's house to play a new game, so I'll see you after dinner."

"You're not going to stay with me today?" I feel like a deflated balloon thinking about spending the day alone.

"Nope, and you have to be nice to Mom and Emma. I helped them plan your birthday surprise and it's going to be awesome!"

I let the chocolate melt in my mouth. I don't really want to spend time with Emma and Mom. I thought that after Emma had moved out things might get a little better between Mom and me, but they didn't. The best way to avoid a big fight is to avoid her, especially if Emma is coming for a visit.

"Ok, I'm going to walk over to Carter's. Happy Birthday, T!" He gives me a quick hug and runs through our yard and down to the street.

"You want me to walk you?" I yell down to him. The passing cars whiz by and he just waves. I don't know if he heard me and is ignoring me or just didn't hear me at all, but I wave back and sit down to eat the last bite of the Reese's in the dirt. Tabby Sue walks over and rubs against my legs. I scratch his dirty ears and think about giving him a bath. Like all cats, he hates it and since he is getting so old I just leave the dust and dirt on him. He crawls into my lap and sniffs the wrappers.

"You want some, Sue?" I ask him.

His dark striped ears twitch and he begins to purr.

"You know, today I'm fifteen. I think it's going to be a good day."

I take a bite of the chocolate cake and pretend that I like it. I'm sitting at the small square table made of mahogany that Dad built during his first marriage. Years later, when I'm moving out, he tells me that the table was one of the only thing he salvaged from that relationship and the one thing he will hold on to if he ever decides to leave Mom.

I keep my legs tucked up under myself to avoid the cold floor. Beneath the dirty carpet must be a slab of concrete. Often owners of homes will use this instead of a regular foundation to save money, but it makes the floor unusually hard and the cold never seems to seep out of it.

I swirl my fork around in the dark brown frosting. I don't like chocolate cake, and won't until I'm six months pregnant, but it is Mom's favorite so that's what we have for my birthday.

"So, we were going to take to the mall and let you buy a few shirts with the money Dad left for you, but we had a better idea." Mom says, through a mouth full of cake.

"What?" I ask. I was hoping just to take the 20 bucks up to my room and save it for a while. Maybe I could save up enough money to buy an old computer so that I don't have to use the ancient typewriter to write my stories on.

Emma smiles and picks up her cup. After she gulps some milk down, she says, "Well my friend just got her bellybutton pierced and it looks pretty cool. I would get it done, but I like to sleep on my stomach, and it would probably bug me too much." She pushes her dyed black and pink hair out of her face. I think about how she's a good liar and how it seems to just flow out of her without any problem. I know that the reason she won't get her bellybutton pierced is because she's 250 pounds.

I think about saying this to her, so she gets mad and leaves me alone, but I don't feel like fighting. Especially since Dad won't be coming home from his conference for another two days and Finn is still at his friend's house. I don't want to be alone without backup in case things were to get ugly.

"Umm, no I don't think I'll do it." I drink the rest of my water and squish the cake with my fork. Maybe if there are lots of little pieces, I won't have to finish it and I can go back up into my room.

"Come on, it will look so cool and I bet the boys will like it." Emma smiles at me in what she must think is a convincing way.

I think about Alex and almost laugh imagining a proper Mormon boy liking, let alone looking, at my bellybutton.

"No I don't really like piercings and stuff, plus I wanted to buy a new shirt with my money."

"I'll pay for it." Mom puts her cup of milk down and licks her fingers.

"I don't really want to do it." I look at Mom's face and try to show how sincere I am. Her face is bloating from some new pills she has been taking. It makes her cheeks puff in perfect half circles and press against her eyes which in turns makes them squint perpetually.

"Tara, it will be so much fun. We can all drive down there together and afterwards we will take you to the mall to get some clothes," Mom says.

I think about how dumb a piercing is. I don't want some weird guy to shove a needle through my bellybutton. It seems like such a stupid thing to do to your body.

"I'm not 18 though so I won't be allowed to do it." I hope they believe me and leave it alone.

"Let me call my guy. I bet since Mom says its ok, he'll do it!" Emma grabs the phone and dials a number from memory, which isn't surprising considering how many earrings she has in and the two lip rings that stick out of her mouth. I start to feel anxious as she goes into the other room to talk.

"Mom, I really don't want to do it."

"Shut up, it's cool. You'll like it," she brushes some crumbs off of her shirt and smiles at me, "It'll be fun to go down there together. Just us girls."

I've never been included into their little group before, and I wonder what it will be like. Maybe I'll just go and chicken out at the store and then we can all go shopping together. The intense desire to belong and to fit in with them takes over. I want to know what it is like to laugh and joke with them. They seem like they have a lot of fun together and I have always wanted to be a part of that.

I wonder if a bellybutton ring really will make me more attractive. Maybe if I get it I won't have to actually show anyone because the knowledge that I have one will make me attractive.

I don't know if I really want to go through with it though. I don't like pain or blood too much. I've never had the desire to shove metal through my body. Before I have made up my mind, Emma comes back.

"My guy said he would totally do it, but we have to leave now so we are there before he gets off," Emma says while grabbing her purse and jacket, "Come on!" She walks out of the door and I hear the boards of the deck squeak under her weight.

"Girls Road Trip!" Mom yells and follows Emma.

I take a deep breath and try not to think about what's going to happen. For the first time ever, Mom and Emma want to spend time with me. I'm part of their exclusive group and will finally know what it's like to have a good time with them.

I pull on my shoes and run after them slamming the door.

The car takes a few minutes to warm up and, before I'm ready, we're cruising down Highway 18. The highway has four lanes and weaves in and out of the San Bernardino National Forest. The ugly plants on the side of the road look dead but are only in a state of dormancy because of the lack of water. After a few rainstorms or a big snow fall the plants all seem to come alive with vibrant colors and fill the air with their strange aroma.

I giggle nervously as we get closer and closer to the bottom of the mountain. Mom turns on the radio and an old Beatles song comes on.

Emma and Mom start to sing, and I alternate the lines with them.

"You say yes,"

"I say no,"

"You say stop,"

"I say go, go, go,"

"Oh no," they scream into the wind before laughing.

"You say goodbye. I say hello. Hello, hello. I don't know why you say goodbye, I say hello," I keep singing even though they have stopped. It feels strange to be included with them, almost like breaking the rules, but I like it. I feel happy and can't stop smiling despite the dread I feel about what they want me to do.

Emma tells Mom where to turn and before I know it we are pulling up to a dingy little tattoo parlor. Mom parks on the street and I feel nervous about getting out of the car. The neighborhood is dirty and just a few houses down there is a big group of people just sitting around outside. Graffiti covers the entire side of the tattoo shop and loud music floats out of a broken looking car.

"Let's go do this!" Emma laughs and pushes open the door. I follow her and try to keep my hands from shaking.

Behind the desk a man with tattoos covering all the exposed skin, except his face, smiles at us.

"You didn't tell me you were going to get here so soon," he says, smiling at Emma. I can't understand him very well because of his strong Latin accent.

"We wanted to make sure we got here in time."

"It'll be twenty bucks. She can follow me to the back while you guys get the cash out."

He pushes aside a red curtain and holds it open for me to follow him. I don't want to admit to anyone that I don't want to get it done so I follow him without saying a word.

The hallway is dark and he leads me to a little room at the back. There's a chair in the center of the room and a tiny counter and sink along one of the dark red walls.

"I'll need you to lift up your shirt and you can just stand while I do it." He slips on some blue gloves and smiles at me.

I just pretend this isn't happening and pull my shirt up. I try not to look at the needle that he pulls out of some plastic or at the piece of gauze he sits on the chair.

"Alright, I'm gonna sit down and when I pierce it make sure to keep breathing. I had a girl pass out the other day because she was holdin her breath."

He pulls my hips closer to him as he sits down. I fight the urge to twist away and try to focus on breathing.

"Here we go," his hands are cold and I close my eyes.

I breathe in. And out. And in. And then it feels like my stomach is on fire. I open my eyes without thinking about it and see the three-inch curved needle sticking out of my stomach.

He reaches for a little ring and pushed the needle out with it, replacing it. He screws on the top little ball and looks up at me.

"Breathe!"

I take a deep breath and realize that I had been so focused on watching him that I had stopped breathing. I smile and take a few deep breaths.

"Hold this on it so you don't drip blood everywhere and sit down for a second." He hands me the gauze and starts to clean up. As I sit down pain shoot through me. I adjust the angle that I'm sitting at so I'm straighter and don't bend at the belly too much and hurt the new piercing.

The man mumbles some instructions on how to clean it and what to watch out for before leading me back to the front room. Mom and Emma demand to see it.

I pull my shirt up. They both laugh.

"Does it look alright?" I freeze and wonder what could have gone wrong. Maybe he did it wrong and now I'm stuck with some weird metal ring in my stomach that looks stupid.

"Yeah, it's fine," Mom says as she hands the man a twenty, "Let's go shopping."

We all pile back into the car. I try to be careful with my new bellybutton ring, but every bump in the roads makes it ache.

"Do we have to go shopping today?" I ask.

"Yeah, that's what we said we would do," Emma says.

"But the piercing hurts and I want to just lay down."

"Stop being such a baby. You're fine," Mom says, turning up the radio.

They start to sing together again, and I look out of my window. I don't feel like shopping anymore. I wish they would just listen to me.

We park in the front entrance of the Inland Center mall and they both climb out.

"I really don't feel like shopping, Mom. My stomach hurts and I'm tired."

"Just get out of the car." Emma rolls her eyes and waits for me.

I climb out and slam the door, hard enough to shake the car.

"It's my freaking birthday! I don't want to go shopping. Just take me home." I know that part of my anger is because, somehow, I'm not part of their group anymore. Sometime after getting my piercing, the wall has gone back up dividing us.

"Stop being so annoying. We're trying to have fun with you are you're ruining it."

"I didn't even want to come down here in the first place."

"You wanted to get your bellybutton pierced," Emma says it like it is the dumbest idea in the world.

"You are the one who told me I should get it done! It's probably because you're too fat to. He probably couldn't even find your belly button to pierce it!" I yell. I'm angry with them for not taking me home, but I'm angrier with myself. I can't believe I let them pressure me into getting it done and I can't believe I thought that I would ever be in their group. I should have known better.

"You're such a bitch, Tara. We do something nice for you to try to help you be more popular since you're such a loser and you think you can just yell at us?" Emma gets in my face.

I know she hates it when I call her fat, so I keep doing it. "Get your fat ass away from me. Can you even bathe properly? You stink." I want her to be just as upset as I am.

"Let's go Emma. Let's just leave her here." Mom hold the keys up in the air and swings them at me. "You're an ungrateful little brat. Maybe if you have to figure out how to get home, you'll be nicer to us."

I look at her face and can tell that she is not kidding. She is going to leave me in the middle of San Bernardino with no way to get home. I don't even know what street we are on, let alone how to navigate the 20 miles through San Bernardino, which is one of California's most dangerous cities, back up to the mountains. The mountains alone are nearly a mile high. Walking up the highway would be incredibly treacherous.

I snatch the keys from Mom's hand and run into the mall. I know that they can't leave without me now. I run through the crowds and duck into the nearest store. It is a small boutique that has a lot of expensive looking clothing on display. I browse around the back of the store and keep a look out for Mom and Emma. I don't want them to find me right away because they will still be mad. Hopefully they will shop around a little bit before they find me so that I can convince them to take me home.

I shove the keys into my pocket and hear a crunching sound. I pull out a crinkled twenty dollar bill. I take a deep breath and leave the boutique looking for a cheaper store so I can buy a new shirt.

I wander into Forever 21 and immediately see a white shirt with small, multicolored hearts covering it. I like how long and flowy the shirt is. I pull it from the rack and hold it up to my shoulders. It looks like it might fit.

"Can I help you?" A young woman with an apron and name tag asks me.

"Um, can I try this on?" I don't know what the policy is on trying clothes on, but I want to make sure it fits before I spend my birthday money on it.

"Sure. The dressing rooms are in the back." She points for a second before folding the clothes on the nearest table.

I take the shirt to the back and quickly throw it on over my sports bar. I look at myself in the mirror and think I look pretty. I pull the shirt off and whimper as my new bellybutton ring catches on the seam and gets yanked.

I carefully put my own shirt back on and bring my new shirt to the counter.

"That's all for you?" the same girl outs the shirt in a bag and while I nod.

"It's 17.98."

I hand her my twenty and she gives me back the change. "Have a good day!" she says.

I smile and leave the store, triumphant. I have never gotten a new shirt before or been able to buy anything at the mall on my own. Being fifteen is going to be great.

"Tara Muller?" a man says behind me.

I spin around. A security guard has his hand on his hips and looks angry. He has grey hair and is so round I wonder if he would be able to fit in a car comfortably.

"Yes?"

"I need you to come with me."

"Why?"

"Are we going to have a problem here?" He takes a step towards me and I realize just how tall he is, "Just come with me before anything bad happens."

I don't know what will happen if I don't follow him and I don't really want to find out. I trail behind him through the mall and try to ignore the looks I'm getting. He leads me to a weird little hallway and opens a small door that says security.

The room is just large enough to fit two desks and a few chairs.

"Take a seat." He motions for me to take an old metal fold up chair in front of his desk. I sit down and clutch my shopping bag to my stomach. Even though it irritates my new piercing, I'm too nervous to loosen my grip.

"We have reports of a Tara Muller matching your description being involved with Grand Theft Auto. Are you Tara Muller?"

"What are you taking about?" Grand theft auto? I don't even know what that means.

"Are you Tara Muller?"

"Yes."

"How did you get here today?"

Then I understand. Mom and Emma must have been so mad that I ran off with the keys that they called the security guard.

"My mom and sister drove me down here, but they were going to leave me here because I was bugging them so I grabbed the keys so they couldn't ditch me down here." They could have just come to find me and I would have given the keys back. But they were mad that I called them fat and ruined the day. Now they are going to try to get me in trouble. I take a deep breath and try to remember to just tell the entire truth and everything will be alright.

"You stole the keys from them and when you did you injured your mother's hand. That's assault, not to mention Grand Theft Auto."

"My mom wasn't hurt at all and I didn't steal anything."

"By taking the keys and preventing them from leaving you basically stole the entire car. I could have you arrested."

I feel helpless and angry. My stomach feels like I have been on a roller coaster and I hope that I don't throw up. "I took the keys so that they wouldn't leave me here. We live in the mountains and I have no way of getting home." I try to keep my voice steady and calm.

"You could have used the pay phones."

"I didn't know I had money until I put the keys in my pocket. Can I just talk with my mom?"

"The women didn't want to confront you because they thought you would be violent."

I can just hear Emma telling lies to the guards. She's so good at it that they must have believed her.

"I just want to go home."

"Give me the keys and we will try to work this out. But I'm warning you, any funny business and I will be calling the Sherriff department and reporting this as an assault and theft case."

I hand him the keys from my pocket and follow him back into the main hallways of the mall. He walks slowly to the other side, past the crowds of people staring, and makes his way to the fountain. Sitting on one of the benches I see Mom and Emma each eating a burger from McDonalds.

They see me and stand up. Emma is smiling and has a drop of ketchup stuck to her chin. I don't say anything about it. Maybe if I look down and sad they will just take me home. I stare at my feet and try to look upset by shuffling around.

"Excuse me, Ma'am? I have your keys and was wondering if you would like me to press charges?" The security guard's voice is smooth, and I wonder if that is how he talks to everyone until they are in trouble. In his office he just barked at me.

"No, as long as she gives me the keys and we go home right now."

"Mom! She attacked you and threated to leave us here. I think we should have her spend the night in jail." Emma's voice is high pitched, and I glance up at her to see her face. She looks genuinely worried and I wonder how she got so good at acting.

I'm furious that she is blaming me for doing exactly what they were going to do. As the security guard hands the keys to Mom, I see Emma smile at me behind his back.

I know that losing my temper will just make things worse, so I wait. I store it all up so that once I'm in the car, I can scream at them.

"Do you feel safe enough to take her home?" he asks mom.

"Yeah, I guess. As long as she goes straight to her room and doesn't try to cause another incident." Mom looks at me.

"I'll go to my room. Just take me home." It's getting harder and harder to keep from yelling so I focus on a little bug that is crawling near my feet. It's a little black beetle with a shiny back.

Mom and the security guard chat for a minute before he turns back to me.

"I have given your mother my phone number. If you do anything else today, she will call the police and then me. I will give them a report and you will serve time, understand?" He scowls in my direction which cause his face to be filled with wrinkles and weird bumps. I wonder if he likes having control over people and if that is why he took this job.

I nod and hope that he will just leave.

He does. He waves to Mom and Emma and waddles back towards his office.

I glare at my family.

"Let's just go. Don't even think about yelling Tara, or I swear I'll have you taken away." Mom walks towards the doors and Emma follows, shoving me in the process.

I march ahead of them to make sure I make it to the car. I don't want them to jump in and leave me here anyways. I hold onto the handle while Mom unlocks her door, and because of the automatic locks, my door clicks too. I jump inside and slam it.

"Come on T, calm down. Why don't we turn the radio on and sing again?" Mom sounds happy and I fight the urge to slap her. I don't want to calm down. I don't want to see them or hear them, and I definitely don't want to pretend that I belong with them anymore.

"Just take me home." My voice is deeper than normal, and I try to keep it from shaking with anger.

"Bitch," Emma says.

"Take me home."

I can see Mom roll her eyes from the rearview mirror and she slams the car into drive.

I sit in the back seat for almost an hour and think about how dumb I had been to think I was part of their group. I decide that I will never be included and that I should just be happy that I have other people in my family that I like.

The same Beatles song comes on the radio, but instead of singing along, I hum happy birthday to myself.

32 Weeks

The living room is warm, and all the lights are dim. The fire cast a yellow glow into the faces of Alex's family. Everyone is talking and laughing while Ground Hog's Day plays in the background. The conversation had started out with a discussion of politics, as it always does, but it wound its way to funny stories from everyone's childhood. It has already been close to an hour and the stories just keep coming.

"Who wants to hear a story about Alex?" Alex's mother says, smiling.

"Oh, I do." I say. I look over at Alex, who looks embarrassed, and I smile mischievously.

"This was back when you kids were little. I was in my bathroom getting ready for my nightshift at the hospital when Jessie came into the bathroom followed closely by Alex, who stood by the door. She told me that sometimes when she uses the bathroom her urine burns. I saw Alex cock his head to the side and could almost see the gears turning as he thought. I told Jessie that if it happens again, we'll go to the doctor because it could be a bladder infection. She left the bathroom, but Alex stayed standing by the door still absorbed in his thoughts. I turned to finish getting ready when Alex came up to me. I looked down at him and he looked very serious and concerned. He said, with a little quaver in his voice, 'Mom, sometimes when I pass gas... it's hot.'" Everyone bursts out laughing, including Alex who is laughing the hardest.

As the laughter dies down Alex says, "Want to hear my favorite story of you Mom? It's not a funny one though."

"Yes, please," she says.

"I remember how we used to go on car rides together. We'd drive around and look at houses or we would go down to your work together. I remember how we would talk about your job and all the weird pathological issues you've seen in labor and delivery. You know I think it was those talks that made me want to go into Biology."

Alex pauses for a moment and I can tell he's getting emotional. He continues, his voice shaking and tears in his eyes. "Anyway, the thing I remember most fondly about those trips were when you would hold out your hand and say, 'Do you know how much I love you?' and I would grab your hand and say, 'How much?' 'More than anything' was always the response."

I squirm in my seat. Alex wipes a few tears away and his mom smiles. She tries to say something but can't. She just shakes her head. I look to the other members of his family and realize that most of them have tears in their eyes.

I excuse myself quietly and walk past the kitchen and into the small bathroom. I close the door and cry until someone knocks.

"Just a minute," I call.

"Hey, it's me. Can I come in?" Alex whispers through the door.

I splash some water on my face and pretend that I was just washing it. I open the door while patting it dry with a towel.

"What's wrong?"

"Oh, I just had to go pee. You know being pregnant is kind of annoying. I swear I pee every 30 minutes."

"You looked upset out there," he motions towards the living room.

"Yeah, it was just that story about your mom and you. It was..." I lose my voice and can't talk. Tears well over and I burry my face into his chest.

"Oh, Babe..."

"I'm sorry. I'm sorry I'm being so dumb." I wipe my eyes and pat down his shirt with the towel. "Sorry for crying. It's so annoying. I swear it's these stupid hormones." I try to hold back the tears but can't. "I'm sorry," I sob.

"Tara, it's ok to cry." He rubs my back.

"No, it's not. I'm sorry. I'll stop now." I hold my breath for a minute and focus on not crying.

"Tara, it really is ok to cry. It's probably good that you cry at that story. It means you're going to be a good mom."

"It means I'm weak."

"Do you think I'm weak? Or my dad? Or my brother?"

I shake my head. The men in his family are a strong group, even if they are free about showing their emotions.

"Crying is a good thing, it means you feel something," he says, "It means you're connecting to those around you. It's alright if you cry."

"I just can't believe you had a relationship like that with your mom. Your family is so different." I stare down at my round stomach. Currently, it looks like I shoved a ball under my shirt. It's perfectly round for just a moment before one of the girls begins to move. Something pushes out towards my hands. It must be an arm because of how long it sticks out of my belly. It's nearly 2 inches long before it disappears back inside, almost like the disappearing of a whale tale back into the deep.

I rub the spot, gingerly, where the baby disappeared. There is still movement, but nothing pokes out again. I kind of wish, despite how weird it is, that she would push her hands towards me again. I can't wait to hold each of their little hands. The love I feel for them is indescribable.

"Honestly, I worry that I'm not going to have those stories with the girls. The ones that everyone laughs at or cries at. The ones that just feel so…" I try to think of how to explain the difference between what I grew up with and what I just witnessed in the living room. "So wonderful," I finish.

"Babe, you will. You already have. I just saw the way you looked at that creepy hand reaching out from inside of you. You are totally in love." Alex pulls away from our hug and smiles at me.

"I want to be able to have so many good stories that everyone can sit around and talk about them for hours. I just really want us to be all together and just happy."

"We will. You are the perfect person for those girls to call mom. They choose you for a reason."

Midnight Run

The Victoria's Secret entrance is filled with a giant cutout of a model in red and black lacy lingerie. The amount of skin showing makes me feel awkward looking at her. I go to the second door to the side and feel a little more comfortable with the sweatpants and regular t-shirts. Loud music is playing as I browse the pajama sets.

"You should just wear your old stuff, it's not like it matters what you look like," Mom says, tapping her foot, "You're only sixteen."

"I want something new. I'm sharing a room with two other people and don't want to have holes in my pants and stuff." I walk to the next display and look through some of the long night dresses. They remind of when I was little and I would wear Dad's old shirt for night dresses. I pass by the section and look at some tank tops. I know I need something cute for my first wind ensemble trip away from home. We are staying in the Disneyland hotel for three nights while we perform concerts and record music in their studies for movies. I'm excited for the trip and the free time in the park, but I'm more excited that Alex is going to be there.

We promised to spend as much time together as we could, and I want to make sure that when I go down to breakfast in the morning, I'm in cute pajamas and not a ratty old shirt.

I find a light green tank top and matching shorts that look cute. They're not as revealing as the lingerie in the front of the store, but they still make the model look great in the photo display.

"You won't fit into that." Mom says from behind me.

"They're in my size." I check the tag and find the M indicating medium.

She folds her arms over her chest, and I wonder if she is feeling self-conscious in the store. She always yo-yos back and forth with her weight and right now she is on the heavier side. Before I can feel bad for her she turns and glares at me. "Just because you can squeeze into it doesn't mean you should get it. You're too fat to wear something like that. Just wear your old stuff so we can go."

"I'm going to go try it on. Thanks for your help." I walk to the back of the store and try to keep my head held high.

The dressing room is pink like the rest of the store and the assistant promises to come back if I need anything. I block Mom's voice out while I close the door. The lights are bright and I wonder if the pajama set is a good idea but slide into it just to see. The tank top is tight, and the shorts hit the top of my thigh, just a few inches longer than regular underwear. I look into the three-section mirror and am surprised to see that I look nice. The light green color of the tank top contrasts nicely with my dark brown hair and even make my eyes look a little green. I check to make sure that I don't have any rolls around my stomach area, but I can't see any.

A light knock on the door makes me jump.

"Someone's in here" I call out.

"I know, I came back to help with the fitting." The dressing room assistant's voice seeps under the door. I've never been to a store like this, but I guess it's normal.

I open the door and she comes in. Her bright blonde curls bounce around as she looks at me from every side.

"This is a beautiful set on you! It really brings out your hourglass figure." She says, making me spin and I wonder what an hourglass figure is.

"If you are looking for something sexier, I have a red and black corset that would be killer one you."

"Oh, no! I just need a something to sleep in on my next trip," I say, horrified at the thought of me wearing anything like the model in the front of the store.

"Well, if you want to sexy this one up even more you could go bra-less with it. And we have a little white robe that you can cover up with too in case you need to be a little more modest."

"The robe sound like a good idea."

"Perfect, I'll go get one and bring it to the register for you. Just come up when you're done shopping and I'll ring you up." She smiles and closes the door quickly behind her.

I get back into my regular clothes and make my way to the front register. Mom is waiting near there looking at the lotion and body wash.

"I'm not paying for you to look like a slut."

"I'm paying for myself."

"If you want to look like a fat stripper then go ahead. I'll be in the food court."

She barges her way to the entrance and leaves. I smile at the assistant that helped me earlier and try to pretend like everything is fine.

"So, is it just the pajama set and the robe?"

"Yeah, that's it."

I watch as she wraps it in zebra print tissue paper and place it in a big square bag. I hand her the cash and hope that the trip will turn out just like I hope.

The hotel entrance is bright and filled with about one-hundred students. Mr. Jefferson stands at the front desk and occasionally glares at us all when we get too loud.

"I can't wait to go on Pirates of the Caribbean. It's one of my favorites. What about you?" I ask Alex. He's standing next to me and smiles.

"I'd rather just hang out in the hotel or go to the movies or something."

"We have free access to Disneyland and California adventure for the majority of three days and you want to go to the movies?"

"Yeah, I don't really like lines and people in Disneyland can get crazy."

"You'll come on Pirates with me through, right?" I ask.

He rolls his eyes. "I guess I will." His voice is low, and I know he's teasing me.

I smack him in the stomach and laugh. "Sorry to be such a bother."

"I'd rather you bother me than someone else." He looks up at me, surprised, and then looks away quickly. I can feel my checks get red and wonder if he meant to say that out loud or accidentally let it slip.

"Atten Hut!"

"Rim!" We all snap to attention. Our echoes travel through the halls and I can see several startled guests near the counter watching us.

"Alright, I have the room lists and keys. Rules are simple. The boys are on the second floor. The girls are on the third. No boys in girl's rooms and vice versa. I don't care what you guys do in the park or downtown Disney. You are not to go anywhere else but the parks and downtown. Curfew at midnight. That means back in the hotel at midnight. If you are not back before then the cops will be called. If we find you, you will be sent home and suspended. You can be in the lobby or the balcony until one am. Then I will come around and tape the door shut after a head check. If that tape is broken before I check it at six am those in the room will be sent home and suspended. Be on time to our performances. Be professional. We are here as guest to the park. They are paying us with the free tickets." He looks over to where all the drummers are standing and narrows his eyes a bit. "Do not embarrass me. Now line up with your roommates and get your keys."

The room is filled with shuffling feet and bags. Alex nudges my shoulder with his and says, "See you later." He disappears in the crowd and I look for the girls in my room. I see Hana and Lei standing in the middle of the line and join them.

"Don't get Alex suspended, Tara." John wiggles his eyebrows at me as he passes to join some of his friends. I roll my eyes at him and look back to Hana. She's smiling at me.

"Just don't get caught with Alex this weekend."

I pull on my hair. "Come on, we're just friends." My voice sounds convincing, but the blush that creeps into my face gives me away.

"Yeah, and I'm not a banana." She laughs.

"A banana?"

"You know, yellow on the outside but white on the inside?" Lei says pointing to Hana's arm.

"Hana, come on. Is that a real term for Asians?" I don't know if she's being honest or teasing.

"It is. It's actually a bad thing. It means you're Asian but not Asian enough. That you try to act like white people more than your Asian heritage. It's like being called an Oreo if you're black."

"Do people really call you a banana?"

"In Japan, yeah. It's even worse for me because I'm actually part white. They don't like having someone who's mixed in Japan. It means you're not pure." Her face is blank, and she looks down. I know she is actually bothered by this, so I smile.

"That must be why our people got along so well," I say.

She looks confused for a second before smiling back. "That's true. The Germans and the Japanese do like eugenics. That's why we're such good friends. We just understand each other." We laugh and I wonder if someone were to overhear us would they know we are joking or think we are serious?

"We do." I say seriously. I never have to tell Hana if I'm upset or how I'm feeling, she just somehow knows. And I think I can tell how she is feeling too.

Lei rolls her eyes. "You understand each other because you're both white."

Before we can say anything Mr. Jefferson motions for us since we are next in line. "Names?" he asks.

"Muller, Kato, and Lin." I say.

He checks us off the list and hands me three room keys. "Don't lose them. You each get one."

"Let's throw our bags in the room and get a few hours in the park. Then we can go to dinner in downtown." Hana pulls on my hand and leads me to the elevator.

"Why not just eat in the park. There is that restaurant that's part of the Pirates of the Caribbean ride." Lei says, pushing the button.

"You need reservations and it's probably expensive." I only have 40 dollars for lunch and dinner for the three days. Breakfast is included with the hotel and I didn't want to ask dad for any more money. I'm going to eat at the fast food places in downtown Disney so that I don't run out of money.

"Yeah, and downtown has some cool places."

Lei rolls her eyes. "Whatever, I guess I'll just order some of the food from the room then. I don't want to go to some fast food place."

We ride the elevator in silence. Hana and Lei are friends and I put up with Lei because of Hana. Sometimes, when Lei says annoying things, we just suffer through the awkward silence for a while.

We walk down the hall and find our room on the corner. The door won't open for me, so Lei shoves me to the side and opens it. "Have you never used a key card before?"

I ignore her question, not wanting to admit to it, and go inside. There are two full size beds and a plush chair as furniture. A small dresser has a TV on top and the little closet is filled with hangers. I drop my old duffel bag on the floor in the closet and peak into the bathroom. It's small and matches the beige and white colors of the bedroom. The toilet is right next to the shower and the small sink and mirror fill the rest of the space. The small bottle of complimentary shampoo and condition won't be enough for the whole trip for all three of us. I've never stayed in a hotel before and I wonder if we can request more.

I walk back into the main room. Hana is sitting on one of the beds while Lei has all her luggage spread out on the other.

"I'm taking this bed. You guys can share the other one or one of you can sleep on the chair." Lei unpacks her clothes and starts hanging them up in the closet.

"We can share since you're so little." Hana pats the bed next to her and I jump onto it.

"What ride should we go on first?" I ask.

"Let's just go explore. Maybe we'll bump into some cute trumpet players," Hana whispers so that only I can hear her.

I raise my eyebrows at her and pretend I'm mad.

"You coming, Lei?" Hana asks.

"No, I'm going to unpack and take a shower. I'll see you guys later."

I pull Hana out of the room before Lei can change her mind. I don't really like spending time with her and any chance to get away from her is a chance I'll take. I hate the way she acts better than everyone. It brings out my insecurities.

"Let's just walk around Main Street and look at the shops. My brother used to bring me these cherry candies from the candy store that were really good, and I don't even like cherries. If we find them, I'll buy us a bag and we can sit on the bench and eat them all." Hana links arms with me.

"Sounds good to me." We walk towards Disneyland together without speaking. For the first time in my life I feel like someone knows me really well and the silence doesn't become awkward.

The back streets in Disneyland are busy and full of characters running to get to their next place to meet the guests. Bell and her Beast run by and wave at us while we follow each other in a single file line. The Disney escort speaks into a megaphone and points out interesting spots to look at. I always wondered how the workers get around without being seen. The tunnels and back streets are still kept beautifully painted and filled with decorations, even though only workers see it. The security guards stationed every hundred feet watch us carefully for any cameras or cell phones. We were told we could be fined, and our device would be confiscated if we were to take photos behind the scenes.

After passing a few more restaurants and staging areas for the parades we file into a large square building. After going through the inner room and through another set of doors a beautiful stage greets us. The chairs are plush with red velvet and the music stands are all different colors. The chairs are all set up in a half moon shape and face an enormous screen.

Mickey waves at us before Walt Disney himself appears smiling in black and white. There is no sound so I can only guess he's telling us about his park in the film that plays. Mr. Jefferson walks up to the director's stand and motions for us to sit in our regular spots, as if we were in our own dingy band room.

"The director of our music program will be out in just a few moments. He's going over the score to our latest film. Take this time to warm up and get comfy." The escort sits down on a couch in the back of the room and takes out his phone.

"Get warmed up. In five minutes, we play the fight song." Mr. Lee's voice is higher than normal, and I wonder if he is just as nervous as I am to be recording movie music with the head of the Disneyland musical division.

After putting my clarinet together, I set the case down beneath my chair. I glance towards the back and find Alex. He's across the room in the center, surrounded by the rest of the trumpets and brass section. His hair is slightly out of place and looks like the wind had been strong, but I know it's from him running his hand through it. He laughs and knocks the music off the boy's stand that is sitting next to him. He runs through a few scales before he notices me watching him.

He smiles. Putting his trumpet down in front of him he mimics clarinet players by raising his eyebrows, puffing his cheeks and swaying in circles while wiggling his fingers. Clarinet players may sway a little, but the rest is just an exaggeration. I roll my eyes before squeezing my eyes closed, making my mouth a tight thin line and pretending to play a trumpet. I pretend to strain and point my imaginary trumpet high in the air before opening my eyes. Alex is glaring at me. Before he can tease me again, the light tap of the conductor's wand hits the music stand and I turn to face Mr. Jefferson.

After playing music for most of the classic movies and even a few new songs for the mini movies Disney is making, we pack up. I have never struggled so hard to play music before. The timing had to be perfect or the technicians wouldn't be able to sync it properly to the movie animation. We had to play the sections over and over until we played it quickly enough and then we had to play it a few times after that to make sure there were no mistakes.

The exciting thing is that Disney promised to make DVDs of our shoot and send it to us in a few weeks. We get to actually watch small clips of movie with us playing in the background.

"Glad that's over." Alex's voice pulls me from my thoughts, and I turn to see him stand next to my chair.

"Yeah, if I had to hear one more toot from a trumpet I would die."

"Really? Because the most irritating thing that I heard was the screech of a dying cat coming from a clarinet."

I push him gently and walk with him towards the back doors. He pushes me back and I run into the door frame.

"I knew clarinet players were a little clumsy, with the swaying and all, but I thought that only lasted while you played." He laughs. It's loud and deep and makes me smile.

"Shut up, that was all your fault." I try to push him back, but he expertly steps just out of reach. "So, are you going to hang out with me today or ditch me like yesterday?" I ask. I try to keep my voice even and not give away how bummed I was to not see him yesterday at all.

"I didn't ditch you! Mason, Ben, and I just stayed in downtown for a while looking at the shops and then went back to the hotel and watched TV."

"How fun," I say, with a fake smile.

"It was kind of boring," he admits before laughing a little. It's not his regular laugh though. It's a little higher pitched.

"What?" I know something is up. His smile goes from ear to ear and he looks guilty.

"Oh nothing. Just something from last night."

"What happened? You didn't make Ben wet the bed or anything did you?"

"No, but that's a good idea." Alex reaches over and pulls me closer to him to avoid stepping into a pothole. I like the feel of his warm hand on my arm, but he takes it back quickly and rubs it through his hair.

"So, what happened?" I ask making sure my ears are covered with my hair so he can't see them getting red.

"We were flipping through the channels on the TV and Mason stopped on like a volleyball game or something. And suddenly, this girl takes off her shirt. I thought they would blur it out, but they didn't! And then she started running around topless."

"So, you guys watched some naked girl run around together?"

"No! Mason and I started yelling and trying to change the channel, but Mason dropped the remote and Ben was just sitting there watching it. We finally turned the channel and just started to laugh because it was so weird."

"Poor Ben. That will probably be his only time seeing a topless girl." I joke.

"It was really weird. I hope the hotel doesn't charge the room for that or something."

"Mr. Jefferson would love to see that on the bill." I laugh imagining how a teacher would react to seeing that on his student's bill.

The escort finally leads us back to the regular streets of Disneyland through a special hidden gate. I look for Hana but before I find her, she pushes Alex to the side.

"Since you ditched her yesterday, I get her all to myself today." She looks at Alex and drapes her arms around my shoulder.

"Oh, uh that's fine." He kicks a pebble around for a second before looking at me. "Mason, Ben, and I are going to go to the movies later. At like 9. Do you want to come?"

"Sure. Where do you want to meet?" I ask.

"Just the movie theater in downtown Disney. Hana can come too, if you want." He says the last part, looking at her.

"I will. You guys will need a chaperone after all." She smiles mischievously before pulling me away from Alex.

"So, your first date, huh?" She asks, just out of ear shot of Alex.

My heart starts to beat fast and I wonder if it is a date. "No, we're just going out as friends. With a group of friends. Right?"

"Sounded like a date to me."

I walk to the movie theatre with Hana and a group of other girls. I run my fingers through my long hair and try to stay calm. I'm pretty sure we are all just hanging out as friends, but the possibility of a date with Alex makes me feel like I'm going to throw up.

I check my watch to make sure we aren't late and Hana bumps into me a little.

"Stop fidgeting. We're just all going to hang out. Just make sure to sit by Alex, alright?" she puts the strand of hair I have been playing with behind my shoulder and smiles. Her brown eyes squint a little and make her look more Asian than normal.

"Ok." I say.

"And make sure you don't wander off to his room or are late for curfew. Mr. Jefferson is so mad about Haru's hand that I think he would just kill you instead of suspending you."

"What happened to Haru?" I ask.

"Stupid Steven slammed Haru's hand in the door of their room. Haru had to go to the hospital and get ten stitches and won't be able to play music for the rest of the trip."

"Oh my gosh! Is he alright now?" I think about Haru and how he has always been so sweet to me. He never treats me like his little sister's annoying friend. Every time we see each other he has a huge smile on his face and honestly wants to now how I'm doing. He is one of the most genuinely good guys I have ever met.

"He's fine. But Mr. Jefferson is in the worst mood because he had to spend six hours last night at the emergency room and has lost his best trumpet player. Just don't get caught getting too snuggly with Alex."

I roll my eyes at her. Before I know it, the theatre looms up before us. I immediately look for Alex and find him standing near the doors with a few of his friends. He waves and before I get to him, I pretend that I'm completely calm.

"Hey." I say.

"Hey Tara, how're you?" Mason, Alex's best friend, gives me a hug before I can say anything.

"Good. What are we seeing tonight?" I ask.

"*Night at the Museum 2*. You can sit between me and Alex." He rubs my shoulder for a minute and holds the door open for me. I walk through and pull Alex in behind me.

"So, that's Mason." I say quietly. I have never spent much time with him. He's always super friendly and very popular, but whenever we have a class together I spend time with Alex instead.

"Yeah. He's a good guy."

"Kind of cuddly, isn't he?" I ask, watching as Mason hugs each of the girls in our group and compliments them.

"Yeah, he's not doing it to be a creep though. He's just a really nice guy. He was basically raised by his mom and grandma and so he's always complimenting girls and hugging them. It's just who he is."

"That's sweet."

The rest of the group joins us and starts to buy their tickets. Alex and I fall to the back of the line and as we approach the ticket woman I get more nervous. I wonder if he's going to offer to pay or not. And if he does offer, does that mean it's a date?

"Do you really want to see Night at the Museum?" he asks, raising his eyebrows.

"Not really, but what else is there at this time?"

"*Angels and Demons*, the sequel to *The Da Vinci Code*." There is a twinkle in his eye, and I laugh.

I look above the window and see the starting times for each of the movies is just a few minutes off each other. "We're just going to ditch everyone?" I whisper.

"Why not?" he looks at the group and back at me. "You really want to hang out with them all night?" he grins.

"Ok, let's do it."

He grabs my hand and pulls me to the window. I wish he didn't have to let go, but he reaches for his wallet and says, "Two for the 9:30 showing of *Angels and Demons.*"

He hands the cashier a twenty and we rejoin our group just for a moment. The theatre showing our movie is the second to the left. I wonder how we're going to explain it all, but Alex grabs my hand and pulls me that way. We break away from the group and run inside. Just before the door closes, I see Mason and Hana watching us with big smiles on their faces.

I ignore them and follow Alex up into the isles. We find a seat towards the top of the bleacher like seats and sit right in the middle of the row. The huge screen plays previews and reminders to turn off all cell phones, but we don't pay attention to them.

"I really liked *The Da Vinci Code* and have been wanting to see this one. I hope it's good."

"It's pretty good." Alex puts the arm rest down on his side but leaves the one up in-between us so that we can sit closer to each other.

I scoot just a little closer to him before saying, "You've already seen it?"

"Yeah, but I remember you talking about it a while ago. I thought it would be fun to go with you," he looks at his feet, "I mean, it's got to be better than the stupid museum movie, right?"

I laugh. "I hope so."

The opening credits start to play and I lean back in my seat. The lights dim and I can feel Alex sliding over towards me until our shoulders touch. I lean gently on him and try to focus on the movie instead of him.

The opening scene is full of mystery about the Popes death, but I can't focus entirely on it because I notice Alex's slow breathing and the faint smell of old spice. Our sides are pressed together, and I realize that I've never been this close to a boy before, especially a boy that I like. I take a deep breath. Hopefully Alex can't tell how nervous I am. I force myself to focus on the movie and only allow myself to think about what is going on in the scene.

After about twenty minutes I feel Alex's head on my shoulder. I look over at him and notice that he's starting to fall asleep.

"Psst," I whisper.

"Hmm?" he says, without opening his eyes.

"You're really falling asleep?" I ask. I'm a little disappointed that he's falling asleep. I'm too nervous to be so close to him to even pay attention to the movie very well. Maybe he doesn't like me as much as I like him.

Mom's words start to fill my mind.

"You're so annoying, no wonder you have no friends."

"You're so weird."

"You look fat. You should stop eating."

"No one is going to like a book worm who wears glasses. You're just so ugly."

"I'm only falling asleep because you're really warm and I feel really comfortable." Alex says, nuzzling my shoulder a bit.

"Is it really that comfortable laying on my bony shoulder?" I giggle, Mom's words erased from my mind with Alex's quiet whispers.

"Yeah, I like it." He takes a deep breath and sighs.

"Why don't you lay in my lap so you're actually laying down?" I sit Indian style with my legs crossed and put my sweater in my lap like a little pillow.

He lays his head down and faces the screen. Before I focus on the movie again, I wonder what I should do with my hands.

I can't lay them in my lap since Alex is there and I don't know if I should set them on his back or hold them above him. I hesitate for a minute before I just lay them on his back. I look back at the screen and don't recognize anything, but it doesn't matter.

The end credits roll and I twirl a lock of Alex's hair in my fingers. I started running my hands through his hair halfway through the movie and soon after he started snoring. I look at his peaceful face, not wanting to wake him. His strong jaw line and soft looking lips make me blush a little and I'm glad the lights are off in the theater.

I gently touch his face and whisper, "Alex?"

He doesn't move.

"Alex?" I say a little louder and rub his back.

"Hmm?" he stretches and looks up at me. "Hi," he says, his voice hoarse from being asleep.

"The movie's over."

"Did you like it?" he takes a deep breath and sits up.

"Yeah, it was pretty good. It followed the book pretty well too, and that's always nice." I pull my sweater on and am happy that it's still warm and smells like him.

"Yeah, I think they did a pretty good job on it too." He pulls me to my feet and our hands linger together for a second before he pulls away.

"Do you know what time it is?" he asks.

"No, let's just check in the lobby."

He leads the way and we walk in silence, enjoying each other's company.

"Oh no," he says, "We've got to go!" He grabs my hand and pulls me through the doors. He's running and it's hard for me to keep up. I don't ever run and I'm way shorter than him.

His long strides and calm breathing shows his years of soccer and cross country training.

"What's wrong?" I wheeze.

"It's 11:50. We have to get back to the hotel." He holds my hand and weaves through the crowds that still fill the downtown Disney streets. People stare at us and jump out of our way, but I'm too afraid of being suspended to care what they think. If we are late for the hotel curfew we will get in huge trouble. I run next to Alex and focus on breathing.

I try to keep running, but soon my side hurts and I can feel my lungs straining. I hope my inhaler is in my bag.

"Alex, we have to stop." I pull on his hand.

"We can't," he says, "We have to make it."

"Alex, I can't breathe!" I stop moving all together and he skids to a stop.

"Ok, let's just speed walk for a while." He holds out his hand and I grab it.

"What if we're late?" I ask.

"We'll just say that the movie started late because of technical problems or something." I don't think that will work on Mr. Jefferson, especially after Haru's injury. But I don't say anything.

He turns down the street the hotel is on and looks back at me. "You think you can run the rest of the way to the hotel? It's about a quarter of a mile."

I take a few deep breaths and it feels like my lungs are on fire. "Yeah, I'll try."

We start to jog together and then break out into a run. Our footsteps fall to the pavement at the same time and create our own beat to follow. The cold night air cools the sweat on my face. Just when my lungs seems to stop working the hotel comes into view. Alex lets go of my hand and puts on a burst of speed. He reaches the door and holds it for me as I hobble through.

We speed walk to the lobby and find Mr. Jefferson sitting on a couch with a few of the chaperones.

"Oh, it's you two," he smiles, "Get upstairs."

I can't believe our luck. It's after midnight and we didn't get in trouble at all. Alex walks me to the elevator in silence and we only start to laugh once the doors are closed.

I laugh until I start coughing and Alex pats my back.

"You alright, asthma girl?"

"Yeah, once I get my inhaler from my room."

"Why didn't we get in trouble?" he asks.

I think about the smile Mr. Jefferson gave us before sending us to our rooms. I wonder if my crush on Alex is obvious to everyone. I shrug my shoulders and say, "He probably knows we weren't doing anything bad."

"Yeah, maybe." Alex says.

The elevator doors open on his floor and he leaves, but just before the doors close, he stops them with his hand. "You want to talk for a few minutes on the balcony before it's time for the room curfew?"

"Yeah, let me just get my inhaler and shower really fast. Meet me outside of room 312 in 10 minutes?"

He nods and lets the doors close.

I race to my room and am thankful to see Hana and Lei already in bed. That means I can take a quick shower and not have to wait for one of them.

"Where did you and Alex go? And why are you so late?" Hana whispers from bed.

"I'll tell you later. I have to meet him outside in a few minutes."

I grab my pajamas from my bag and ignore her teasing grin. The water is cold in the shower so I jump out and quickly drag a brush through my hair. After drying off, I look at the pajama set I bought.

I want to look good, but Mom's words float back into my head. I throw the tank top on without a bra and realize that it is way to revealing to go out in. I slip my bra on and the shorts and make sure that I'm covered in the mirror. I know I don't look like a fat stripper, but I wonder if even still it is too revealing to be around Alex. I know he's Mormon and I've heard they are a pretty conservative group. I consider putting the robe on, but Alex knocks on the door and I tip toe to it.

I leave the door slightly open and meet him outside. He's in pajama pants and a black shirt that looks like an old soccer shirt. He must have showered because his hair is wet and he smells like soap.

"Wow," he says, "You look beautiful."

I freeze for a second. No one has ever told me that I am beautiful before. Mom's voice fills my head again, but Alex's voice drowns it out. "It makes your eyes look almost green," he says taking a step closer to me looking into my eyes. He's so close that I can smell his toothpaste and feel his warmth. I imagine kissing him for a second before I feel my face turning red.

My heart is pounding, and I sit down before he can get any closer. He sits next to me and we look out over the city together.

Crestline Girl

I lean against the wall outside of math class waiting for Alex. I fidget with my shirt, hoping the old fabric doesn't look too dingy. The white shirt with multicolored hearts is still one of my favorites. It's one of the only things I have ever gotten for myself at the mall. I feel just a little more confident in it.

I hear some laughter at the end of the hall and turn to watch Alex and a group of friends walk up. He's the tallest of the group of guys. As his friends pass me and go into the room, he lingers outside with me.

"Hey," I say.

"Hey." He smiles and quickly looks down at his feet.

"You want to sit by me today?" I motion towards the door.

"Sure."

He holds the door open for me and I walk through. The class is full and loud. I pick a seat at the very back. I usually sit in front so that I can pay attention. I don't like math and it always seems like I need to spend a little more time on it then the others in my class. I generally get the correct answer, but the extra time it takes me means that I can't sit near my friends so that I'm not distracted.

Alex takes the seat directly in front of me and swivels around in his chair to face me. I pull out some paper to take notes and to doodle on. I draw a squiggly line and look up to see Alex's big blue eyes watching me.

"What?"

He takes out a pencil and makes my squiggly line into a snake. "Nothing." He says before drawing a spiral next to a straight line.

I make the spiral into a tornado. "You were looking at me weird." I draw a two-storied house with the straight line as one of the walls. Then I draw a large S.

Alex draws a fat elephant with my S as the trunk. He smiles at me quickly and then draws a square.

"What are you thinking about?" I ask.

Alex starts to turn his own square into a 3D box.

"Hey, it's my turn to draw. Your turn to answer the question." I push the tip of his pencil away with mine. I try to turn the box into some sort of weird monster with legs.

"I was just thinking about Disneyland." His voice is low and quiet. The huskiness of his voice makes me feel warm.

"What about Disneyland?" I ask, keeping my eyes on the page.

He pushes my pencil out of the way and draws a little stick figure. "Just about how I really liked going last time." He draws another stick figure person next to his first.

"I did, too." I wish we could go back. It has been a month and a half since that trip. We have been spending as much time together as we can. We flirt, and it seems like we are dating, but neither of us has asked the other officially.

"Hopefully the next trip will be just as nice."

I glance up into his eyes. There is just a bit of yellow right around his iris that looks like sunlight bursting out from behind some clouds. Just as the blush begins to creep into my cheeks Mrs. Cooper calls Alex's name.

"Huh?" he asks, looking to the front of the room.

"I was just wondering if you would like to tell me the answer to the example on the board." Her annoyance seeps through her voice despite her friendly smile.

I look at the board and don't recognize a single thing. There are about twenty variables and a single number in an equation that fills the length of the entire white board. Alex stares at it for just a moment before saying, "The answer is 6x + 3h-5."

Mrs. Cooper glances at the board before gruffly saying, "Correct. Tara, can you answer the next example?"

"I would need way more time." I say, quietly.

"Alex, please face forward. You may be able to glance at any question and figure out the answer, but others can't and need to pay attention." She glares at us a moment before continuing her lecture.

He turns to face forward. I pull out a new sheet of paper and begin to copy the material off the board. None of it makes any sense. After about ten minutes Alex is facing me again. We quietly play our doodling game, forgetting everything else.

When Mrs. Cooper gives us a handout of practice questions for homework I begin to get nervous. The sheet looks like a foreign language. And she mentioned that there would be a quiz on this material on Monday.

"Want to be my partner?" Alex asks, holding both of our handouts.

"Only if you don't mind teaching me how to do them."

"We only have a few minutes left in class. Do you want to just come over tomorrow and I can tutor you?"

"Really?"

"Only if you want to." He says, smiling.

"I'll have to ask my dad. I don't think we have anything planned though, so it should be fine. What about your parents?"

"I'll ask them tonight and then call you later."

I smile at him and start to pack my things away. It isn't until we are walking out of class that the nerves kick it.

"You sure you know where his house is?" I look outside at the unfamiliar neighborhoods.

"I used to work up here as a security guard before you were even born. I know these streets, T." Dad turns left onto yet another unfamiliar street.

Alex lives up in Lake Arrowhead. Lake Arrowhead is more expensive than Crestline, and caters to tourists. It is often a place where celebrities will vacation to get away from the city and enjoy the lake and natural beauty of the San Bernardino National forest. I never spend time in Lake Arrowhead.

"I just don't want to get lost." The further we get into the area, the larger the homes become. Some have gorgeous lawns in front, which must cost a fortune to upkeep in the mountains where that type of grass is not naturally found.

"Where did you say his house was again?" Dad asks.

I read him the address and wait anxiously as he takes another turn.

"Is it in a gated community?" He asks.

I look down at the paper Alex handed me after school yesterday. It has the address and bellow it there are four numbers. I guess they could be the code for a gate.

"Uh, maybe? There are a few numbers here that could be for a code."

"Why did you have to go make friends with someone who lives in a gated community in Lake Arrowhead?" Dad rubs his hand through his hair. I can tell that he's agitated.

"What's wrong with that?" I ask.

"He's just not on our level. We know the real world, ya know?"

"What does that even mean?"

"It means that those people probably don't even know how hard the world really can be. They know nothing about living paycheck to paycheck. They don't know how to survive."

"Dad, you don't even know them. Just because they live in a gated community doesn't mean that they haven't had hard lives before. Alex is my best friend." I don't know why Dad is acting so strangely. He doesn't normally judge people before even meeting them.

"I just don't want you to get to close to them, ok?" He glances at me and reaches for my hand. "I don't want them to judge you because you come from a hard-working family and you don't live in a secluded area. And don't tell them about your mom."

"I won't." I feel a pit in my stomach. I wonder if our differences will really matter to Alex or his family.

As we pull up to a gate, I start to feel almost sick. Dad punches in the code and slowly drives in. We pass beautiful estates. Large homes with river rock exteriors, huge green lawns, three and four car garages, and beautiful landscaping that looks all professionally maintained. The homes are the likes of which I have only seen in movies before.

"Definitely do not tell them anything about our house. I used to patrol in this neighborhood when I worked security, and some of them are worth millions of dollars. That one," he points to a large stone covered cottage that looks like it belongs in Europe somewhere, "has a wine cellar that is as big as our entire house almost. The owners gave me a bottle of wine once that was so old you wouldn't believe how it tasted."

We drive down the street a little more and stop in front
of a large driveway. The white and tan house is large and well
maintained. The long driveway leads to a three-car garage. To
the left of the house is a small incline that is filled with different
plants and trees. I can make out a few rose bushes sprinkled
throughout the yard as well.

"This is it. That house has got to have at least five bedrooms
in it and it looks like it sits on an acre lot. The three-car garage
will probably fit our entire lot inside of it." Dad looks up at the
house and whistles. "Don't tell them anything about us, ok?"

"Do you really think they would treat me any differently
if they knew we didn't have money like them?" I try to sound
offended, but my voice is quiet and filled with new insecurities.

"I don't want to find out. Just study math and then call me
when you need to be picked up." He gives me a quick kiss on
the cheek before I get out.

"Love you." I say, quickly grabbing my math book and
folder before turning to face the house.Dad's words buzz in my
head while I stand on the driveway. I wonder what a Crestline
girl is doing here.

I take a deep breath and walk towards the house. There's a
little pathway that leads around the house and I assume that it
leads to the front door. The pathway is covered with tiny blossoms
from the trees surrounding it. The shade feels good against my skin.

As I pass a little bend I nearly run into a man kneeling
in the dirt by the pathway. Hiking boots peek out underneath
the rolled-up bottoms of his beat up old jeans and a big straw
hat sits on his head.

"Oh, sorry!" I take a step back, embarrassed.

He looks up and smiles at me. He's obviously Alex's father.
They look incredibly similar. Even down to the little crinkle
near his nose.

"You must be Tara!" He wipes his hands on his jeans and reaches out to shake mine.

I smile, shyly. "Yes, nice to meet you." I look down at the area he had been working on. A small hand shovel lies next the base of a tree. Around the base lies a bunch of tan dirt in small piles. He must have been digging a hole.

He notices where my gaze goes and picks up his shovel. "This tree has been slowly starting to lean to one side. I'm pretty sure a gopher has gotten to it, but I wanted to check." He digs a little more and motions for me to look closer.

I kneel in the dirt next to him and examine the tree and the hole. It's leaning slightly to the right. But I don't see any tell-tale signs of a gopher; no mounds of dirt being pushed up around the tree or the rest of the little hill.

He scrapes some dirt out from around the tree and says, "There it is! The gopher tunnel!" He points to a little tunnel with the tip of his shovel. I lean down closer and can see exactly where the gopher had been gnawing the tree roots.

"What's around the base of the tree?" I can see weird little wires poking out of part of the root system.

"I wrapped the ball of the tree in chicken wire. If a gopher takes a liking to my tree, it's supposed to keep them away from the most important part of the tree. Look here," he taps his shovel against the wires, "If the gopher eats all the way up to the wire, but cannot get through, the tree has enough left to survive and start growing more roots."

"That's amazing. I never knew that little trick." I smile at him.

"It looks like this tree might be alright. I'm going to spray some water in the tunnel and hopefully the gopher will seal it off and not come this way again."

"Do you always work out in the yard like this?" I ask. Dad's words float around in my mind and I wonder if Alex's family just pays for someone to do the work for them.

"Yes, I have done everything you can see out here. I even planted a small orchard in the back yard. I like to add trees whenever we have the money to buy a new one."

His words surprise me. I would imagine that someone who lives in this neighborhood wouldn't have to worry about how much trees cost or wait a while before just buying trees to fill his orchard.

He stands up, shakes off some dirt, and motions for me to follow him. I think about how much work would have taken to get the front yard to look like this. There are decorative plum trees and liquid ambers lining the pathway. Several different types of flowers and shrubs are planted on the small hill next to the driveway. The empty space is filled in with either woodchips or little river rocks that seem to wind around the house and out of sight. It must have taken many hours to get it looking so pristine.

As we walk around the house, my dad's words lose their weight. Alex's dad is so calm and welcoming. I feel my nerves about being at Alex's house dissolve as I listen to him talk about his trees.

He opens the front door and leads me inside. There's a large stairway almost directly in front of the door. Alex's dad takes off his hat and sets it on the end of the bannister.

"If you go through that door, you will find Alex in the living room."

I walk through a room that has several couches and an armoire. I open the door and find myself in another living room. This one has several more couches, a big recliner chair, and it opens into the kitchen.

Alex is sitting at a dining table with a few books around him.

"Hi." I say.

He looks up from his work and smiles. The way it lights up his face calms me. I know that I don't have to worry about being a Crestline girl, or living in a tiny house with my family; it doesn't matter to him.

"How long have you been here?" He gets up from the table and walks to me.

"I've been outside with your dad looking at a tree for a while." I let Alex take my books from me and give me a hug.

"What'd you think of my dad?" He asks, pulling me along to the table.

"He's great. He showed me the tree where the gopher was and taught me about the chicken wire. And then he showed me the front yard and all of his plants and trees."

"Oh, sorry about that. He is really into his plants." Alex leans against the table and runs his hand through his hair. He looks extremely calm and happy. I can't help but notice how good looking he is.

"It was a lot of fun. Your dad is really nice." I twirl my hair between my fingers. "Your house is huge."

Alex sits down at the table and plays with his papers awkwardly. "Yeah, my parents worked really hard to build this."

"They built it?"

"Yeah, it took a while to save up for to buy the empty lot. And then it took a few years to save up for a partial down payment for a building loan. Mom helped design the house and then they started construction."

"How long did it take to build?"

"A year maybe. Or a year and a half. Dad would come here after work and help put things in like the flooring and stuff to help save money and to try to get it done faster."

I look at the blonde wooden floors for any sort of mistakes. They look perfect. "Your dad must be really good with a hammer and some nails to put in floors like this." I smile at him.

"I guess." Alex shrugs. He seems uncomfortable talking about the house. Maybe he is uncomfortable about his house like I am about mine.

"So, I guess we should start studying?" I ask, hoping that a change in topic will make him happier.

"Or, we could get a snack." Alex says.

"A snack seems good."

We leave our math books on the table and walk over to the kitchen portion of the room. Alex opens the refrigerator and rummages around for a while.

"Can you get the toaster out of that drawer there?" he asks, pointing to a cabinet.

I follow his instructions and pull it out. Alex lays bread, tomatoes, cheese, and a bunch of different sauces out on the counter.

"What are we making?" I ask.

"Maybe some tomato sandwiches?" He looks at my faces and says, "Or maybe just cheese sandwiches if you hate tomatoes?"

I laugh and start helping him put them together as our books lay abandoned and forgotten on the table.

"Alex, are you awake?" I whisper.

He doesn't move. He's laying on a pillow in my lap. After eating sandwiches, and talking with his dad a bit, and going on a walk around the neighborhood, he turned on an old movie. *The Sword in the Stone* cartoon is cute and funny. We sat cuddling on the couch until Alex wanted to lay down. I run my fingers through his hair and enjoy being close to him.

I draw patterns onto his back lightly. He rolls over a little and peaks up at me.

"Hey," he says, smiling up at me.

"Have a nice nap?" I ask. I lay my hand on his chest and play with the buttons on his shirt.

"I've never slept better."

We sit without talking for a few minutes. I notice how warm he is and how close we are. I look into his face and notice a few freckles sprinkled near the bridge of his nose. His lips are a light pink and I wonder if they are just as warm as his hands. When I notice Alex watching me, a blush creeps into my face.

His eyebrows furrow a bit. He looks serious and when he leans up on one elbow, I feel my stomach drop.

"Hey," he turns to look directly into my eyes, "I just want you to know how I feel about you." He sits up next to me and leans in close.

"I know." Our faces are almost touching. "Me, too." I lean in a bit more and hold my breath.

The door behind us opens and Alex's dad walks in. Alex immediately leans away from me, rubbing his hair nervously.

"Hey, we have to go to the store for your mom. Maybe on the way home we can drop Tara off at her house?" He glances back at us, "You did study today, right?" His knowing smile makes us both laugh.

"I can tutor you at lunch tomorrow. Deal?" Alex whispers.

"It's a date." I whisper back.

I watch as Alex drives away. He and his dad dropped me off right in front of my house. I was nervous about them driving all the way down into Crestline, but his dad seemed to think the lake and trees made it beautiful. Their small white car turns a corner and goes out of sight.

"You can't tell me you're dating the Mormon boy."

I turn to see my neighbor, Jackson. He's a few years younger than I am. "Shut up. I'm not dating anyone."

He jogs across the street and grins at me. "Well that's good news." He pulls me into his chest quickly and kisses me. I'm so shocked that I don't move for a minute.

Then time speeds up and I shove him away from me. "What the hell was that?" I yell at him.

He runs back across the street towards his house. "I just wanted you to know what you're missing when you're with Alex."

"Touch me again and I will make you regret it." I say before going up my stairs. I can't believe he would do that. I push it from my mind and look for the phone. I can't wait to tell Hana about my tutoring date with Alex.

I eagerly wait for the bell to ring. As soon as it does, I walk out towards the bleachers looking for Alex. I spot him sitting down near the bottom with a few books laid out already. I throw the brown sack lunch bag I brought for him towards the seats. Without looking up, he snatches it out of the air before it lands.

"How do you always know what's coming?" I ask.

"I'm just good like that."

I roll my eyes and sit next to him. "How was your weekend?"

He takes a big bite out of the peanut butter and jelly sandwich I made and smiles. "It was good. You?"

"I liked most of Saturday." I say.

Alex raises his eyebrows and says, "Most of it?"

I wonder if I should even tell Alex about Jackson. Jackson is the kind of guy who does things without thinking sometimes.

I have known him since we were little. Kissing me was just something he did on the spur of the moment. Something that didn't mean anything to either of us. I suddenly wish that I hadn't brought it up at all.

"Yeah, I loved spending the day with you. When I got home, I saw Jackson outside and he was weird."

"What happened?"

"He saw you and teased me a bit and then we kissed."

Alex coughs on his sandwich and sets it down. "You what?" his voice is sharp and louder than normal.

"Yeah, he kissed me for like a second, but it isn't a big deal. I told him off and he went home."

Alex throws the sandwich back into the bag. "That's great." His anger is palpable.

"What's wrong with you? It's not like I kissed him back."

He shakes his head. "I should have known."

"What is that supposed to mean?"

"You're such a slut." His face is red, and his fist are near his sides.

"Excuse me? I didn't want him to kiss me. I didn't ask him to. And when he did, I told him to back off." Guilt floods me and I wonder if it really was my fault. Had I somehow given Jackson reason to think I liked him and would want him to kiss me? Was it, in fact, my fault?

"I don't really care. Everyone says you're not good for me and you know what? They're right. You're just a slut from Crestline and I don't need to waste my time on you anymore."

A Part of Me

I walk through the halls alone, avoiding my regular spots. The white halls and grey tile are all dingy and look more like the hallways of a jailhouse than a high school. I pass laughing students and open doors where lectures haven't started yet. I don't really know where I'm going. Normally during nutrition break I go to the band room and see Alex and Hana, but I haven't done that in weeks.

"Tara!" I look up and smile as Hana runs to me. She wraps her long arms around me and I feel like a little child being held.

"Hey." I smile.

"Still avoiding Alex?" she raises her eyebrows.

"I don't want to talk about Alex." The mention of his name brings his face into my mind. His small smile. Blue eyes. Perfectly combed hair. I miss him and my chest aches.

"You guys always fight over silly things; can't you just be together already? I mean, it's meant to be."

"No, it's not. And we aren't fighting over something silly this time." I pull away from her and wrap my arms around my torso. Maybe if I hold myself the dull ache will go away.

"He just really loves you Tara." Her voice is lower, and she looks sad, "He didn't mean what he said. He was just jealous."

His words echo into my head and it's like he is standing next to me again.

"I don't really care. Everyone says you're not good for me and you know what? They're right. You're just a slut from Crestline and I don't need to waste my time on you anymore."

"Tara?" Hana's voice breaks through my memory and I realize I'm still standing in the middle of the hall with her.

"Alex doesn't care about me. He made that clear the day we fought and every day since then. I can't be around him and I'm sorry that that means not being around you as much anymore. You can come spend the night or something later this week, alright?"

"Really?" she smiles, and I feel even guiltier because the suggestion was just to get her to stop talking about Alex.

"Yeah, any day you want. I'm going to go to English now, can we do lunch on the field again?"

"That sounds great. We'll have a picnic!" She gives me one last hug and walks away towards the band room.

I slowly make my way to the English hall in the back of the school. The huge windows let in sunlight, but since the campus is so windy the hallway is always cold. The few lockers shake because of the wind and it sounds like they are haunted.

I sit down in the empty classroom and pull out my copy of Beowulf. The pages are old and worn from use, but I handle it with care. It's the same copy that Dad would read to me when he was in college and studying for his midterms. I think about Grendel and how one of his major problems was jealousy. I wonder if Hana was right when she said that Alex lashed out because he was jealous. I guess it makes sense, but it still doesn't make his behavior acceptable. If I had wanted to be kissed and encouraged it, then maybe he would have a right to be upset. But calling me a slut because I was kissed against my will is just ridiculous. Anger flares up in me and I hold onto it. I would rather feel anger than the emptiness I have been feeling lately.

I flip to the end of Beowulf and read about his need to ensure that his reputation is good. He decides to go up against the dragon alone to keep his warrior reputation, even though his likely death will leave his people vulnerable. After our fight, everyone heard about Alex calling me a slut. Most people don't even know what happened but since Alex, a good Mormon boy, claimed that I was a slut everyone seems to be treating me differently. The girls all whisper a little when I walk by them in the band room and the guys all joke that since Alex isn't in the picture they want to take me out.

Anger starts to build up again. I slam my book closed and take a few deep breaths.

"Good morning, sunshine."

I look towards the door and see John. I've known him since middle school but never noticed how tall and muscular he is. I wonder why he hasn't been on the football team. He slings his backpack onto the desk next to me and sets a cup of coffee in front of me.

"Have a few drinks of that and try not to take your anger out on it." He sits on his desk and smiles, "Still haven't made up with Brigham Young yet, have you?"

I glare at him from across the coffee cup as I take a drink.

"You know what you need?" John asks.

I take another long drink from his coffee and don't answer. I don't like when people make fun of Alex for being Mormon, even when I'm mad at him.

"You need to get out of here. No reason to keep reading Beowulf, you're like an expert. I remember you babbling about it in seventh grade." He reaches over and takes his coffee back. "Let's get out of here. We can go to the village or back to my place and watch a movie." He takes a big drink and smiles.

"I'm not ditching. I don't ditch."

"Stop being such a perfect student. You always do your homework and are always in class. You've been ruining the curve for everyone since we met because you study like a robot and now that we're seniors it shouldn't matter if you miss one or two classes. Just give yourself a break. Forget about Alex and come have some fun with me."

I flip through the pages of Beowulf and don't notice the eagerness in his voice. It would be nice to be away from school for a while. Maybe I could ditch band next period too, so I won't have to see Alex.

John grabs his bag and mine and heads towards the door. "Come on, let's get out of here." He holds the door open and smiles.

I pick up my book and run after him. His car is in the back-parking lot right next to the English hall. It's an old jeep wrangler that we crammed nearly 10 people in last time we had a movie day at his house. Thankfully it's just the two of us this time so we don't have to be squished and nearly falling out of the car since he keeps it topless. We jump in and drive off before anyone can stop us. He turns into Lake Arrowhead and onto streets I have never been on.

"Where are we going?"

"The village. I want to grab some McDonalds before our movie day."

The car pops out near the village and I wonder if I will ever know the streets in Lake Arrowhead well enough to use the back roads. After he orders enough food for a party, he turns onto another back street and zooms away from the Lake.

I watch the big houses pass by and as we turn onto smaller roads I watch the forest begin to take over again.

"So, I thought we could just rent a movie online and hangout at my place for a while." He pulls into a large driveway and cuts the engine.

"This is Lake Arrowhead?" I ask.

"Yeah, the back part of it. We're kind of by the middle school and kind of by the hiking trails that lead to the desert side of the mountain," he says.

"I have no idea where we are. I don't spend a lot of time up here, I'm just a Crestline girl." Some bitterness fills my voice and I think of Alex. Maybe he was right. Maybe we aren't good for each other because he comes from a wealthier place with big houses and quiet neighborhoods and I come from the working-class town. I think about the houses in my neighborhood and how they are small and filled with either families or drug addicts. There is always a dog barking, usually mine, and people working on cars in their driveways blasting music. I like it. I look around the neighborhood I'm in now and wonder if anyone actually lives around here. It's too quiet.

"You remember where the bathroom is, right?" John asks while walking up a few stairs. He opens the door into the basement and I walk into the familiar home theatre room. The blinds are all closed and a TV nearly the size of the entire wall sits on an entertainment center. There are several overstuffed couches and a coffee table in the room. A stack of folded up blankets sits on the corner of the couch.

"What movie do you want to watch?" He picks up a remote and flips the TV on.

"I don't really care." I say, choosing a spot on the biggest couch and wrapping a blanket around myself.

John sits next to me and flips through the pay-per-view options. I notice his cologne and wonder if it's from Hollister. It smells kind of nice and I think about what Alex wears. Alex's is subtler and smells a little more like cinnamon. I blush a little because of how much I miss how Alex smells. I hope John doesn't notice.

John chooses some random heist film with the typical plot line and big action scenes. He opens the McDonalds bag and passes me random packages. I open them without really looking at them and try to focus on the movie instead of the time Alex and I were at McDonalds. It doesn't work very well and I keep seeing Alex's face in my mind. John sets our sodas down onto the coffee table and we watch in silence for a while.

"Do you need anything?" He asks, scooting closer to me on the couch.

"No, I'm good," I say, watching a car flip over and over and finally exploding into a ball of flames.

"I'm going to go to the bathroom, I'll be right back."

I nod and keep watching the movie. A character in a suit walks through the front doors of a bank and I can't help but see Alex. I went to Alex's Eagle Scout ceremony just before we got into a fight and saw him in his dorky Boy Scout uniform. After the initial ceremony he put his church suit on, and we had lunch at the church building with all his friends and family. I guess he must wear a suit to church every Sunday. It must be a Mormon thing. I remember how nice it made him look. All angles fitted to his nice shoulders and back. The character in the heist movie doesn't seem to pull it off as well. He looks a bit awkward, when Alex looked natural.

"What'd I miss?" John comes back from the bathroom and I notice he's in pajama pants and a muscle shirt. He sits next to me, pulls the blanket over both of us and drapes his arm around my shoulder.

"Nothing really," I say awkwardly trying to remember the last five minutes of movie but can't, "Just typical stuff for a heist movie." I feel guilty that all I can think about is Alex. I was supposed to be watching the movie and be able to report the stuff that John missed back to him.

"Hmm, well since I'm out of the loop anyways, you want to do something else?" his voice is low, and he snuggles into my hair near my ear. His change of clothes hit me then. Why would he change his clothes? Does he somehow think that we are going to have a more intimate night then just a movie night? Is that what he wants? Panic fills me.

"No, the movie is still pretty good." I tilt my head away from him. I feel awkward and very aware of how close John is to me. What once was a friendly snuggle on the couch has now turned into something more. Much more than I want it to be.

"Come on, let me take your mind off of Mormon boy." His hands go under the blanket and pull me towards him.

"John, stop. I just want to watch the movie, alright?" I push his roaming hands away and look at his face. He's so close I can smell his cologne. It's strong and mixed with his sweat. It almost makes me gag. His face looks different; somehow sharper. More serious.

"You know I can help you forget about him, right?" his eyes gleam and I feel like I should get out of here. I don't know what exactly John is planning to do, but I know that I shouldn't be here anymore. He doesn't look like himself.

"If you don't want to watch the movie, let's just go to the village and get ice cream or something." I try to stand up and he pulls me down into his lap. His arms wrap around me and squeeze tight. He turns me around to face him and I can't do a thing to stop him.

His lips find mine and press down. Hard. I try to lean away, but the more I fight the more he seems to like it. It scares me. I finally break away from his kiss and take a deep breath. He rolls over on top of me and pins me down to the couch.

"John, stop," I say.

He pulls his shirt off with one hand and smiles. "You know you like what you see." He runs his hand down his abs and unties his pants. I've never seen him without his clothes on before and he's even more muscular then I thought. He could hit me once and probably send me to the hospital.

I shift my hips and try to throw him off, but he's too big and just smiles. "Just relax. I promise you'll like it." He unbuttons my pants and starts to pull them off. I knee him in the stomach and he laughs.

"I like when you're feisty but do that again and I'll have to punish you." His voice is deep and terrifying. I let my pants fall onto the floor by the couch. Any sort of punishment from him could seriously hurt me. I try to think of a way out of this, but he kisses me again. He tastes like McDonalds food and I turn my face away. He sucks on my ear for a minute and moves down to kissing my neck. He bites me softly, then harder. I push on his chest, with all my strength, trying to get him off me but he barely moves.

"Stop fighting it. Just relax."

"Don't," I say as seriously as I can.

"Shh," he says kneeling on top of me. He pulls his pants off. He already has a condom on.

"I said to stop. I mean it." I try to push him off me, but he's just too big. His hands pull mine above my head and he holds them down with just one of his. He squeezes them tight and when I whimper, he smiles.

"You know you like it rough like this."

His breath is hot and smells like French fries. I turn my face away and focus on the coffee table. I wonder if I were to scream if he would hit me. Or maybe he would like it. Every time I try to get away from him or say no he likes it more and gets more violent. I lay perfectly still and realize that anything I do will fail. He is going to win. He is just too strong for me to fight. I should have known better. I should have seen the signs. Maybe in class he was just a little too eager to get me away. Maybe he has been planning this for a while and that's why we had a group movie night here before. Maybe he has been being my friend just for this reason. I should have realized it before. I should have seen the red flags. I was too distracted with my fight with Alex to notice anything. This is my fault.

"Just enjoy. This is for you."

I take a deep breath and look at the coffee table. My red McDonalds soda cup is sitting right on the edge. I watch the drops of liquid slowly creep down its side and land onto the surface of the table. They begin to roll and catch small rays of light coming from the forgotten television. Just as they hit the corner of the table, I can see a bit of a rainbow in the drop before it falls off the table.

He is everywhere.

I stand at my front door and try to put the key in the lock. My hands are shaking, and John takes them from me. He opens the door but puts his arm in front of it, so I can't go inside. I look down at my feet and focus on my breathing. In and out. In and out.

"Anytime you want to come over, just let me know." He pulls my chin up, so I look at him. His smile starts to fade, and he squeezes my chin a bit harder.

I smile and tilt my head a little, "I will." I say, hoping that it sounds genuine, so he lets me go inside.

He pulls my lips to his and kisses me. I close my eyes and focus on my breathing, but when he starts to get rougher, I kiss him back. I even take a little step closer to him, like I like what he's doing.

That seems to do the trick and he pulls away and walks down my stairs. He honks twice before pulling out of the garage and speeding off down the road.

I stand in the doorway until my knees stop shaking. Before they give out on me, I walk in and head to the bathroom. Locking the door, I start the bath and watch the tub fill up. Each drop of water ripples the rest and it is mesmerizing.

I peel off my clothes and throw them in the trash. I look into the mirror and make sure that the bruises I have can all be covered. The one on my neck will need a bit of makeup, and the ones on my wrists will have to be hidden by either long sleeves or bracelets, but I can manage that.

The front door opens, and my heart starts to race. I locked the door when I came in, didn't I? He couldn't be coming back, I tell myself.

"Tara, you home?" Mom calls through the door.

"Yeah, I'm taking a bath. I'll be out in a little."

I try to make my voice sound normal. I look at my face in the mirror and realize that if she were to see me she would know something was wrong. I practice my smile. I practice making my face look regular and hiding what I'm feeling. After a while I think I can convince her, so I turn away from the mirror and walk to the tub.

I step into the bath and sink beneath its surface. The water is too hot, but I don't change it. I let it burn my skin a little. Maybe it will help me get clean. I scrub with soap until my body is raw and my arms are tired. I let my emotions drain out of me like the water out of the tub and I keep my mind clear. I refill the tub with all hot water again and watch the ripples in the water until the surface becomes smooth like glass.

I try to breathe just enough to get oxygen, but not enough to disturb the water. I lay my head on my knees and stay like that filling my mind with just the image of the water around me.

"Tara, you ok?" Dad knocks on the door and startles me. My heart starts to race, and my hands shake. The movement breaks the glass surface and ripples float away from me.

"Yeah, I'm just getting out. What time is it?"

"It's almost eight. Did you fall asleep or are you reading? It's been like four hours."

I feel surprised that it has been so long. "Reading. Sorry Dad."

The water is ice cold. I pull the drain and wrap a towel around myself. I look in the mirror and see that my lips are blue and wonder if I will get sick. It doesn't matter. I dry off and get into my pajamas. I don't bother brushing my hair. I see my clothes sitting in the trashcan, rumpled and dirty. I take the trash bag out with me and put it outside in the dumpster before going up to my room. I don't want anyone asking me why I'm throwing my clothes out.

I crawl into bed and stay there for the rest of the night. I know I have to be normal tomorrow. I know I have to make everyone think that everything is ok, so for tonight I let myself stay in bed. My cat Tabby Sue and the new cat Honey crawl into bed with me. I burry my face in Honey's fur and cry.

I think about what John stole from me tonight.

He stole my innocence. He stole my comfort. He stole my peace of mind. He stole ever watching a heist movie again without having a panic attack. He stole movie nights. He stole my choice away. He stole my authority.

He will steal moments away from my life to come. My late nights alone, he will steal. My attempt to go to McDonalds again, he will steal. My dreams, he will steal. My first movie night with Alex, he will steal. My first kiss with Alex, he will steal. He stole a part of me.

Always

I keep my headphones in and blast the screamo rock music as loud as I can during the bus ride to school. Nobody bothers me or sits next to me. As the bus pulls up in front of the school, I turn it off and put it away. I take a deep breath and join the rest of the students entering the high school. I walk to the band room and smile as I walk through the doors.

There are about a hundred band kids all standing around in groups eating breakfast and laughing with each other. I see Hana in the front of the room and walk over to her.

"Hana, what day are you going to spend the night?" I give her a hug and smile. My voice sounds a little too high to be normal, but she doesn't notice.

"I was thinking Friday. That way we can stay up late and then go to a late breakfast picnic."

"That sounds perfect." I link arms with her and listen to the rest of the group as they plan their weekend. Everything is going so well. No one can tell that I'm just faking it. No one can tell that I'm not ok. The chatter in the group starts to die away and I look up from my feet. Alex is walking towards us and is starting right at me.

I try to keep my breathing regular, but I can't. I'm breathing too quickly. I take a deep breath and hold it. Hana glares at him.

She looks at me for approval before I nod, and she walks towards another group. The rest of the group follows her, leaving me standing alone. I look into Alex's face and try to smile, but it doesn't work. I haven't seen him in weeks or talked with him, but the way he's looking at me makes me think he knows something happened. I just stare at him until he reaches me. My heart freezes and I know that he can see through my ruse.

Tears fill my eyes and I know I can't hide it from him. I have to get out of here. I turn to walk away but he grabs my elbow. His hand is hot and makes me break out in cold sweats. He turns me to face him slowly.

"Tara, what happened?"

"Let go of me." I hiss at him.

"Tara." His voice is quiet but firm. I stop pulling away from him.

"I can't talk about this. I need to get to class."

He pulls me closer. He doesn't quite hug me, but I am close enough to see the small stiches in his shirt. I feel like I'm looking at another shirt, too closely and that soon the smell of cologne and sweat will become intense. I clench my fists over and over.

"You aren't ok. Please tell me what is going on."

"I can't. You'll hate me. I have to go." I turn back towards the door, but he squeezes my arm a little. "Please?" I beg. I feel like I'm going to throw up or pass out. Maybe even both.

"I'm here for you. Always." He says, before letting me go. I reach the bathroom stall before the shaking starts. I wrap my arms around myself and squeeze tight. I silently cry.

I stay in the bathroom all next period. I apply some new mascara and lip gloss, trying to mask my fit in the bathroom. I put my headphones back in, press play, and let other people's screaming drown everything out.

I quickly walk to my English class. Dreading each step wondering if John will be there. I lean against some lockers across the hall, waiting for class to start. I'm determined to go into the class and pretend like everything is fine. I don't want anyone to know what happened. I don't want John to know how much he has affected me.

The final bell rings and I can't move. I hate that I can't decide to go in or not. I hate that I'm too weak to simply walk through the door. I hate myself.

Instead of going into the classroom, I walk outside and down to the football field. It's unusually foggy and cold, which calms me down. I feel like I'm completely alone within the clouds.

I sit on the top bleacher and watch the swirling fog creep across the football field. I turn my music up all the way. The screaming helps my mind stay blank. I sit there until my iPod dies.

I wrap up the headphones and store it all in my backpack. My fingers fumble on the zipper because of how cold I have gotten. I notice a few raindrops dripping off of the ledge of my seat. I see other drops of liquid dripping off a McDonalds cup. I count each one, trying to ignore everything else. I try to take a breath, but the smell of French fries is overpowering. I gag, then throw up onto the bleachers.

After my stomach is empty, I wipe my mouth on my sleeve. I wonder if I will get in trouble for throwing up. Maybe I should try to clean it. I dig into my backpack and dump a water bottle onto it, washing it away.

I walk back into the building and head towards the nearest bathroom. As I fill my water bottle, I hear someone's deep voice outside. I back away from the sink and lock myself into a stall. Before I can help it, I throw up again.

What is wrong with me? I hate how jumpy and weak I am. I flush the toilet and take a deep breath. I leave the stall and stand in front of the mirror. If John was outside, there is no reason I should act like this. I need to be better. I need to hide my emotions better. I need to be stronger.

I rinse my mouth out over and over. I try to keep my mind blank but when I see myself in the mirror I'm startled. My face is white, almost like I put on the wrong shade of makeup. My eyes have sunk into my face and seem dark. I hate how I look. I adjust my scarf and long sleeve shirt, making sure the bruises are covered. I do not want anyone to see them and guess what happened. I don't want anyone to ask any questions. What would I even say to them?

What if they don't believe me? What if they think I wanted it all and only felt guilty afterwards and came up with this story? What if they think I'm saying these things just to get attention? I did go to his house willingly. I didn't scream or fight much. What if they just call me a Crestline slut? I look into my own eyes and watch my face drain of even more color. No one can ever know.

I check the clock in the corner and realize that school is halfway over. I don't even care. A part of me, buried down deep, is worried. Worried about my lack of feelings about anything anymore. But I burry that part down even further and leave the smell of vomit behind. I walk down the hall and wonder what I should do. I know I can't go to class right now and pretend to be normal.

I pass a few English classes before I see Alex sitting near the door of one. Without thinking I walk into it and feel relieved that Mr. Gregory is teaching. I had him a few years ago and he was always very kind.

He stops lecturing and smiles at me. "Tara! It's nice to see you."

"You, too. I was wondering if I could borrow Alex for a minute." I motion to Alex.

"Of course, you can."

Alex stands up and holds the door open for me. I nod my thanks, and pass him in the hallway. I don't know what I'm going to say to him. I just know that I need to be around him. He makes me feel better. Not so numb and empty.

"Where do you want to go?" He asks.

"You choose." I say.

He reaches towards me and I flinch. He freezes. His eyebrows furrow in thought, but he doesn't try to touch me again. He walks down the hall and through the next. I follow him. He leads me to an area near the old gym that is outside. There are long slabs of concrete that are raised a few feet that make the perfect picnicking spot during sunny weather or lounging areas.

I sit down and place my backpack in between us. I wrap my arms around myself and squeeze. The pressure helps make my chest feel like it won't just crumble in onto itself.

"Tara, what happened?" Alex sits across from me but leaves a good distance of empty space.

"I don't really want to talk about it."

"I know you. I know something big is going on."

"If I tell you, you are going to hate me." Tears threaten to spill out of my eyes, so I look up.

"Nothing would make me hate you." His sincerity surprises me.

"I have been upset since we fought. It's all I can think about." I whisper. He silently nods. "I was upset yesterday and a friend of mine," my voice cracks and Alex reaches for me but stops before actually touching me. "A friend of mine brought me over to his house for a movie day."

The color drains out of Alex's face, but he doesn't say a word. "We turned on a stupid heist movie." I squeeze my chest tighter and try to breath. The cold has seeped into my clothes and make me numb.

"Tara?" Alex's voice is a whisper.

"He went to the bathroom. And came back in pajamas. He started...he took off... he..." tears pour down my face and I look away from Alex. I hate how I cry every few minutes now.

"Can I hold your hand?" Alex asks. He stretched out for mine. I grasp it tightly. His is warm and has a few rough spots on it. I wonder why those are there. "What happened, Tara?"

"He already had a condom on."

Alex exhales loudly. And puts his hand over his mouth. "Did you want to?"

I shake my head.

He plays with my fingers for a minute. "Did you say no?"

I nod.

"Did he do this?" He pulls my sleeve up and gently rubs one of the bruises on my wrist.

I nod, again, unable to speak.

He scoots closer to me and I tense up.

"I'm not going to hurt you. I won't even touch you if you don't want me to."

I look into his eyes. His light blue eyes are clouded. I lean towards him but keep a few inches in between us. He moves my scarf and clenches his jaw when he sees the dark black and purple marks. He puts the scarf back into place, moves my hair around a bit, and leans away from me.

"Who?" I have never seen him so serious before. His voice is full of something that scares me.

"What?"

"Who?" He looks at me and I notice a single tear running down his face.

"It doesn't matter. It's my fault." I say.

"Don't you dare say that."

"I went over. I let it happen. I didn't scream or punch or fight him off."

"It was not your fault. You didn't go there to be raped."

"I wasn't raped. I had sex."

"Did you want to do it? Did you enjoy it?"

"No, but it doesn't matter. I didn't fight him off. I let it happen."

"You did nothing wrong. What if you had fought back? He could have hurt you worse."

I pull the sleeve of my shirt down over my wrist again. I feel incredibly tired.

"Tara, we need to go to the police station."

"What?" I stare at him. "There is no way I'm telling anyone else about this."

"You have to report it so that he can't do this again."

"I'm not telling anyone, anything. And you better not either."

"I could make a report for you or something."

"I will deny everything."

"Why?"

"Because I'm not going to become that girl. I'm not talking about this anymore." I grab my backpack, but Alex catches it.

"I won't say anything unless you want me to. Please, stay?"

I stare into his eyes. "Not another word about this." I say.

"I will do whatever you want me to do. You know how much I care for you."

"Will you just stay with me?" I ask.

"Always."

Intentions

Finn knocks lightly on my door. I roll over and bump into Alex. I'm still not used to him living here, even after nearly three months.

"Yeah?" I say.

"We leave in half an hour."

"What?" I rub my eyes and look at my clock. It's eight in the morning on a Saturday. "Go away."

Finn cracks the door open and it hits one of Alex's boxes. Despite moving in shortly after we graduated high school, he still hasn't fully unpacked yet. I think he hopes to get our own place and get away from my family a bit.

"Get up, lazy butt! I'm taking you to a surprise!"

"Why?"

"You start college next week and I start high school. I want to hang out with you. This summer has been filled with Alex moving in and you guys hanging out." Finn frowns. It's a bit overdramatic.

"You know you like having him here. You guys play games all the time together and watch your lame cop show."

"*Southland* is not a lame cop show!"

"Can't I just go back to sleep?"

"No." He leaves the door open and walks downstairs. I can hear Mom in the kitchen, yelling at someone on the phone. I groan. There is no way that I can fall back asleep.

I roll out of bed and rummage around the closet for something to wear. I throw Alex's socks and a pair of boxers out of the way before I find my jeans.

"What're you doing?" Alex mumbles. He opens his eyes and reaches out to me.

"I'm going to breakfast with Finn. I can bring you something before you have to go to work."

"I just want you to come back to bed." He holds open the blanket for me.

"I really am going to go, but I won't be gone long. I promise."

I give him a quick kiss before walking downstairs. Finn is standing by the door, glaring into the kitchen.

"Let's get out of here. Mom's being crazy again."

I watch her scrub the wall with a sponge. She's holding the phone to her ear with her shoulder and yelling into the receiver. I nod to Finn and open the front door for us.

"So, give me the keys," he says.

"Ha! Yeah right. You don't even have your permit yet, loser." I swing the car keys in front of his face.

"I can get it when I'm fourteen and a half."

"Well, you aren't fourteen and a half yet. You aren't even fourteen yet."

"I will turn fourteen in a few weeks!"

"When you have the legal paperwork, I will let you drive."

"Then you must follow my directions, exactly." He wiggles his eyebrows at me and smiles.

"Whatever, weirdo." I shove him towards dad's car. Dad is already outside in the yard planting new bushes and pruning his existing ones. Knowing Dad, he will stay out side all day long in his yard. He loves being outside and a part of me knows he loves getting away from Mom for most of the day as well.

"Ok, where to?" I climb into the car, throw it in drive, and go where Finn tells me. After driving for fifteen minutes, we pull into the Lake Arrowhead Village. The village is full of shops and restaurants, sits next to the lake, and caters to tourists and locals alike.

"What're we doing here?"

"Just come on." Finn gets out and walks towards the lower village and lake. I lock the car and race after him.

"Are you going to tell me why I'm up so early on a Saturday?"

"We're going out to breakfast to discuss things."

"That sounds ominous."

He shrugs his shoulders and walks into the Belgian waffle house. I have never been here before. He asks the waitress to have a seat outside on their balcony and orders two coffees. I'm surprised at how relaxed and mature he seems.

I sit in my metal chair and face the lake. The water is clear blue and calm today. It looks almost like glass. The bird's reflections float across the surface and make me smile. The waitress serves our coffees and asks if we are ready to order.

"We will both have the French toast with scrambled eggs and sausage," Finn says, without even looking at the menu.

The waitress scribbles it down in her notebook and smiles at him. She looks like she may be a year or two older than him, but she flirts with him anyways. When she leaves, I throw a packet of sugar at him.

"When did that start?" I nod towards the waitress and look back at him.

"I have a way with women, Tara. Don't be so surprised."

"Dude, you aren't even fourteen yet."

"I'm going to be in high school." He looks a little upset. He has always hated being the youngest one in his grade. His birthday just worked out to be at the weird cutoff date. He could have gone into either grade, really. Dad made sure he started school as soon as he could though.

"How'd you know I would want French toast?" It was weird to have him order for me. It seemed like such an adult thing for him to do.

"I know you," he simply says. He adds another sugar to his coffee and sips it.

We sit quietly, sipping coffee. It comforts me to know that we are so close. He was there with me every step of the way growing up and even now. I wish sometimes he wouldn't have had to deal with it, but I'm glad that I wasn't alone. I look into his face remembering when he was just toddler and I took care of him. His face now is on the cusp of manhood. His bright blue eyes have always been large and dominant in his features. His lips protrude a little form his new braces, giving him a permanent pout that I'm sure the girls will go crazy for.

We had both gone down to the orthodontist on the same day. He had recommended that we both get braces to correct a few things. Finn's teeth are more crooked than mine, so I insisted that he get the braces. I know that dad is going to have a challenging time paying for them, and I would rather Finn gets them than me.

Finn notices my gaze and sticks his tongue out at me. The same waitress comes by then and delivers our plates. Finn's cheeks turn a bit pink as he thanks her.

"You going to tell me why we're here?" I say, pouring co-pious amounts of syrup onto my French toast.

"I want to talk to you about Alex." He shoves some eggs into his mouth after covering them in hot sauce and ketchup. The sight of the sauces makes me gag a little. I hate ketchup.

"What about Alex?" I get a little nervous. Before Alex had moved in, I had asked Finn if that would be alright. Finn had seemed excited. They even seemed to be forming a good bond with each other these past few months.

"Well, he's living with us." Finn shoves half a French toast piece into his mouth and chews it.

"He has been for a while now."

"Yeah and he's a totally cool guy. I really like when we game and stuff. But, like, what are his intentions?"

I laugh. "His intentions? You're such a dork. We're dating."

"Yeah, but he moved into our house." Finn's stops eating and stares at me.

"Yeah, and?" I ask.

"Are you guys going to just date for a while or do you want to get married?"

"Why are you being so weird?" I ask.

"You're my sister. I'm going to protect you. If he's just coming around to like hook up and then leaves you heartbroken I'm going to kill him." He says it matter of fact. I think about Alex, who is muscular and fit from years of soccer and running, and then I think about my brother who is on the wrestling team and weighs in at 103 pounds. I almost laugh, until I see that Finn is completely serious.

"He won't do that," I say.

"I just want to make sure that he's going to stick around."

I smile and flick a piece of egg at him. "He's in for the long haul."

"So, he will be my brother-in-law one day?"

"Probably. We don't have a date for a wedding or anything, but we've talked about it."

"Good. If someone's going to date my sister, he better have good intentions." Finn stuffs another huge piece of toast in his mouth.

"Have you been watching like cowboy movies or something where women can't do anything for themselves and men must be protective gentlemen?" My voice is filled with sarcasm.

Finn glares at me. "It doesn't matter. You better be treated well."

"I love you Finn. Alex is a good guy. He treats me like the most important person who has ever lived. He has the best intentions, I promise."

My chest feels warm and a bit heavy. My love for my little brother is overwhelming. I look down at my plate and try to keep my tears at bay. Having him be protective and concerned for me makes me feel good.

"So now that all the serious stuff is over, can we talk about how gross it is that you are flirting with our server who is like way older than you?" I kick Finn from under the table.

"She's hot." He grins.

I roll my eyes.

We drive home with all the windows down, music blaring. We sing along, neither of us knowing all the lyrics. We dance and laugh and tease each other. I pull into the driveway fast and make the tires squeal.

"T, don't!" Finn yells.

"I'm not going to crash."

He jumps out of the car. "It's probably safer for me over here."

"Oh, shut it!" I chase him up the stairs. A scream from the backyard makes us both freeze.

"What the hell?" I say. "Stay behind me." I hold my arm out in front of Finn. I walk towards the backyard, on guard. Finn picks up a large stick and holds it out in front of him.

"Hello?" I call, before rounding the house.

"Help me!" Mom yells.

Finn and I run around the corner of the house. Mom is laying on the ground, clutching her leg. Alex throws open the sliding door and stumbles out, wearing just his pajama bottoms.

"What's going on?" he says.

I shrug. "We just go home," I answer.

"My leg is broken! Oh, God!" Mom yells.

"What happened?" Finn wanders over to her and tries to look at her leg.

"Don't touch me!" she screams.

"Stop freaking out. What happened?" I ask.

"I was hanging up clothes on the clothing line and I tripped over something and fell." Mom rocks back and forth holding her leg.

"Finn, go get the first aid kit. Coach taught you how to wrap ankles and stuff, right?" I ask.

"A little."

"I know how to do some too from sports therapy. Go get some ice and bandages." I kneel next to mom. She's covered in dirt like she had been flailing around.

"Let me see it," I say.

"I can't. It hurts too bad. Just call 911." She moans.

"911 is for actual emergencies. Let me see your leg."

"Get away!" she pushes me.

"Stop it!" I yell. "I'm going to look at your damn leg. Act like a freaking adult."

She stops struggling and lets me get close to her.

"Ok, now straighten your leg out," I command.

"I can't. It is fucking broken. What don't you get?"

"What don't you get? I'm trying to help you. If you keep having an attitude, I will just go back in side."

"No, no. Help me." Her eyes are wild.

"Do what I am telling you to do."

She tries to straighten her leg out but cries out.

"Rotate your ankle."

"I really can't." She starts to cry again. "It hurts so bad."

"Here, T." Finn throws me the medical bag. I pull out some ace bandages.

"I'm going to wrap this around your ankle to help stabilize it. I'm also going to wrap the icepack in place so it doesn't move around. Take off your shoe."

Mom pulls on the lace once, before giving up. "It's swelling too much."

"I'll help." Alex goes around to her other side and unties her shoe. He pulls on it just for a second before it pops off.

"Ok, now hold still." I begin to wrap her ankle with the long strip of cloth. I do a figure eight just like my teacher had taught. I weave the fabric around the ice pack so the it stays directly on her ankle.

"Ok, it's done. Let's get you inside."

"I can't walk on it."

"Well I can't carry you." I look at her 300-pound body. She has been steadily gaining weight for the past year again.

"Then call 911. They can carry me inside," she says.

"I'm not calling 911. Alex and Finn will have to help me carry you inside."

Both guys look at me, surprised. Alex's eyes are wide and he looks down at mom. Finn starts laughing.

"We can't lift her," he says.

"We aren't going to fully carry her. We're going to help her up and partially support her to the living room. She just won't be able to use her injured leg."

I can tell that Alex doesn't think we will be able to. He shakes his head but doesn't say anything.

"Ok, Grab mom's arms each. I will help lift from her front side." We maneuver into place. "Mom, you've got to help us. Just try to stand up on your good leg." We get in close and all take a deep breath. "One, two, three. Go!" I yell.

We all heave. Mom slowly starts to stand up. Finn's face turns red and I can see sweat breaking out on Alex's brow.

"Ok, let's go inside," I say trying to help support my mom. I feel like she is going to fall on top of me and crush me. She's leaning heavily onto my shoulders.

"I can't walk!" she says.

"You've got to hop or something. Just start moving." Alex's is out of breath already.

We awkwardly shuffle towards the door. I prop mom up against the door frame and we all take a break.

"Finn, go inside and bring the office chair with wheels to the door. We can put mom on that and then wheel her around easier."

"Ok!" He let's go of her arm and dashes inside. With every second that passes, mom threatens to collapse and bring Alex and I down with her. I'm sweating by the time Finn gets back.

"Ok, just a couple more hops mom and then we will be done."

She grunts and jumps into the chair. She holds her ankle up in the air and cries.

"Do you want me to take you to the doctor?" I ask. "We can help get you to the car and I'll drive you down." Alex and Finn scowl at me from behind her. They are both shaking with exertion and obviously don't want to help her get down the stairs to the car.

"No. I can just call my doctor and see what he thinks I should do. Can you grab me the phone?"

"Sure." I run into the living room and find the phone on the kitchen table. As I walk back into the back room, Alex and Finn pass me.

"We can't carry her down the stairs. I almost died trying to lift her." Alex whispers.

"If she needs to go to the hospital, have the paramedics come lift her," Finn says.

"I know."

I walk into the back room and hand her the phone. As she dials the doctors number, I get her a glass of water. I throw a few ice cubes into it and bring it back. She's already off the phone.

"What's he say?" I ask.

"He's going to call in a few medicines for me. One for pain and one for swelling. After I take those for a day, if it doesn't seem any better, I need to go in."

"He doesn't want to get an x-ray or anything first?" I ask. Finn walks into the room and leans against the wall.

"Not yet. I can move it a bit now so he thinks I might have just sprained it or something." She wiggles her foot back and forth slightly for a second.

"Ok. When do you want me to go get the medicine?"

"He said the sooner I take it, the better."

"I guess I can go now. I will have to drop Alex off at work first since Dad went down to Home Depot."

"We were supposed to pick up my new wrestling shoes today." Finn says, looking disappointed.

"I can bring you down to get the shoes and then swing by the pharmacy really fast." I punch his shoulder lightly.

He smiles. "Finn and Tara take on the world part two?" He raises his hands for a double high-five.

I slam my hands into his as hard as I can. "You know it!"

"Make sure to take Dad's debit card with you. You know the passcode. Pick up dinner, too, while you are down there." Mom scoots her way over to the door and maneuvers herself towards the living room.

Alex pulls me into the kitchen. "I don't have to be to work for a while. I can watch over your mom and then take the bus up to the village."

"You'd really do that for me?" I look into his eyes and pull him close.

"Yeah." His breathy voice makes me warm all over.

I kiss him passionately for a minute before turning towards the front door. "Love you."

"I love you, Tara."

Finn puts on his new red and white wrestling shoes. He pulls the laces out and re-ties them for the third time while we drive to the pharmacy.

"Ugh, can you stop that already?"

"Aren't they beautiful?" He cradles them to his chest like a newborn.

"They're shoes. You're going to get them sweaty and dirty and nasty." I roll my eyes as he tries them on again, for the fifth time.

"They're going to help me beat people on the mat." He takes them off carefully and puts them back in the box. The way he handles them make it seem like they are made of the most delicate material in the world.

"You're so weird!" I say, laughing.

"You don't understand."

"I'm glad I don't."

He shoves my shoulder a bit. We laugh.

"Let's get these stupid pills quickly so we can get back home. I want to write a little before Alex gets back home from work."

"Still working on that book?"

"It's just a short story. But it's really fun to write."

"Yeah, who wouldn't want to work on a story on their summer break." He rolls his eyes at me.

"You just don't understand." I think about how the pen and paper feel beneath my hand. How satisfying it is to get the bulk of a story written down so that you can see it.

He smiles. "I'm glad I don't."

The drive up the mountain is beautiful. But a bit long. I switch lanes during the turns so that I can maintain my speed throughout the entire trip. Because it's in the middle of the afternoon, the roads are pretty empty.

I can't shake the feeling that I'm forgetting something. I started feeling like this at the bottom of the mountain. I check the gas tank cover again in my mirrors. It's snuggly in place.

"I have my wallet, right Finn?"

He pulls my bag closer to his leg and digs through it. "Yeah, it's right here."

"Can you make sure Dad's card is in there?"

He opens my wallet and nods his head. "It's all here. What's wrong?"

"I feel like I'm forgetting something. I don't think I forgot anything today though."

The rest of the drive it bothers me. Finally, at home, I put the car into park and turn the engine off. Something starts to dawn on me. Why would the doctor be in his office on a Saturday? Why would he prescribe medication without seeing her?

"Finn, let me see Mom's pills."

He hands me the white pharmacy bag without question.

I pull out the two bottles of medication. One is labeled as Vicodin and the other I don't recognize. I check the side effects and the warnings on the labels, but nothing is out of the ordinary.

"What are you looking for?" Finn asks.

"I'm not sure. Something just seems off."

I look at the date filled. "Hey, what's today?" I ask.

"Uh, I think it's the sixteenth."

I look back at the bottle and it hits me. The bottle of Vicodin was filled on the twelfth. I check the other bottle and see that it was also filled four days ago.

"Mom said that her doctor called in the prescription and that it would be filled today, right?" I ask.

"Yeah, why?"

"These were filled four days ago. And the doctor's office isn't even opened on Saturday, I bet."

"Who is the doctor listed on the bottle?" Finn asks. His voice is deeper than it had been moments before. He understands what is going on now, too.

"Dr. Cho."

"The dentist?"

I nod my head. "Yeah, it looks like she didn't even call anyone today."

Finn shakes his head. He picks up his shoe box and slams the door closed.

"Finn?" I call after him. He waits.

"Let me handle it up there, ok?"

"She lied about it all."

"Yeah. But I want to catch her at it. Just follow my lead."

"Sure," he says.

I walk up into the house with him. Mom is laying on the couch with a pillow propped under her foot. She has several bowls of snacks near her feet and a few water bottles as well. She has the remote and is flipping through channels. She turns and smiles at me.

"Hey Teester! How'd it go down the hill?" she asks, putting down the remote and turning to face me.

"Fine. It is a good thing that your doctor was in the office on a Saturday."

Her smile fades.

"I got you some Vicodin and then something else I don't recognize."

Her eyes follow the bag like a dog's follow food in the kitchen. "Thank you so much, honey. My ankle is really bothering me." She holds out her hands expectantly.

"You know, what's the name of the doctor who prescribed these again?" I ask.

Her eyes narrow. "I'm not sure. They have several different doctors in the same office."

I nod and smile. "That makes sense. You know, it's a good thing that I rushed down there to get these. The pharmacy has a policy that if medication isn't picked up within five days they put it back on the shelves and you have to refill it with authorization from the doctor."

Her mouth becomes a thing line and she doesn't say anything. I can see that she knows that I know. She is angry.

"What're you talking about, T?" Finn asks in a mock concerned tone.

"I'm talking about how these medications were filled four days ago and that if they weren't picked up by tomorrow mom would have to call the dentist and have him authorize the prescriptions again." I watch Moms face as I speak. She glares at me. I think about that phrase 'If looks could kill' and finally understand the meaning. She looks like she wants to beat me.

"The dentist?" Finn pretends to be surprised.

"Oh yeah, did Mom not tell you that her medication was from the dentist? She lied to us so that she could get drugs."

"What the hell is going on?" she asks.

"Yeah, Mom. What the hell is going on?" I let my anger fill my voice.

"Nothing," she sneers.

"Did you even fall today?" I ask.

"Why don't you go up and read your books and leave me alone. Your voice is irritating."

"No, you're going to tell me what I want to know, or these pills are going in the trash." I smile at her savagely.

Mom ignores me and turns the TV up. I walk over to her and take the remote from her hand. "You're going to talk to us." I flip the TV off and throw the remote onto the floor.

"Fuck you."

I laugh. "You know what I think happened?" I turn to Finn. "She wanted some drugs again. She had an old prescription from the dentist. She called it in but couldn't figure out a way to get them because we have been watching her medicines lately. So, she pretended to fall and then talked us into going down to get the meds." I watch mom squirm. I'm so angry that I like it. She sits up and throws the pillow from under her foot at me.

I smack the pillow away and lean down into her face. "That's what happened, didn't it?"

"Get the fuck out of my face." She stands up and walks into the kitchen. She isn't limping at all.

"So, you made Alex, Finn, and me carry your fat ass into the house for no reason. You screamed like a maniac and were acting like you had broken your foot just to get drugs. What the fuck is wrong with you?" I yell.

Finn puts his hand on my shoulder, but I shrug it off. I stalk mom into the kitchen and get into her face again. "You didn't care that we took time to wrap your ankle up and carry you into the house. What did Alex do for you while we were gone, huh? Did he put the fucking pillow under your leg for you and get you those snacks?"

"Get away from me before you regret it."

"You're just a pathetic drug addict."

She slaps me. My cheek stings and it takes every ounce of self-control not to hit her back. I step back and smile.

"That's fine, druggie. Watch this." I go into the bathroom and open her bottle of pills.

"What are you doing?" she sounds worried. She barges her way into the bathroom just as I dump the pills into the toilet.

"No!" she screams. She rushes to the toilet and looks into the bowl. The pills are already starting to disintegrate. White streaks begin to creep away from each small capsule.

"You bitch!" She yells. She kneels and looks like she is going to scoop them out. I reach over and flush the toilet.

"Don't you ever use me or Finn to get your drugs again."

I don't look at her as I walk out of the bathroom. I grab the car keys and pull Finn out of the house with me. I know that we need to get out of there. Maybe permanently.

37 Weeks and 4 Days

I support my large belly with my hands and waddle towards the car. I feel like I'm in a dream. We're on our way down to the hospital to deliver the twins. We decided to get induced because baby B is finally head down. Hopefully, the twins will cooperate, and we can have an easy and natural delivery. The thought of labor scares me, but what comes after is terrifying.

Alex opens my car door and helps me to lower myself inside. I look back at our little red house and wonder what it will be like to bring home two babies. I hope they will be comfortable and happy here. Alex throws the hospital bags into the trunk and takes his seat. We sit in silence for a minute before he turns to me.

"Are you ready?" he asks.

"No." My hands tremble and I try to breath normally.

"What're you worried about? The delivery?" he reaches for my hands and holds them tightly in his own.

"No, if it gets too much for me to handle I can always get an epidural."

"Then what is it?"

"We're going to have two tiny little souls to watch over. To feed, change, burp, and care for. Every single thing they need will have to come from us. If we don't do something right, they could die." The responsibility of it all feels crushing.

"Yes. But we also get to grow and love these two little girls. We get to help guide them through this life and try to teach them from our mistakes. We're so blessed to have them in our lives."

"I know. It's all just so daunting. I feel like I'm doomed to mess up. What if I ruin them?"

"Babe, you're the best mother I have ever met. You've carried two babies at once while finishing a degree, moving, caring for your brother, and looking after me. You've been sick most of the time. You've kept the babies in for longer than the doctor thought was possible for you. You're an amazing mother already."

I watch as one of the girls' elbows presses out of my stomach. The sight and feeling still freak me out a bit. I rub my stomach and the little limb disappears back into my belly. "I just love them so much. I want what is best for them."

"And that is you." Alex pulls my hands up and kisses them.

His sincerity seeps into me and calms me. I begin to think about what the girls will look like and how sweet they are sure to be. I can't wait to hold their tiny hands and finally snuggle them.

"Let's go have some babies." I smile.

The drive down the mountain is beautiful. A light rain begins to fall and just as we pass the last turn, I see a double rainbow streaking across the road. Alex looks at me with a gleam in his eyes. I know that he's excited to be a father and finally be able to hold his girls.

Checking into the hospital takes no time at all and before I'm completely ready, we're in the delivery ward. We have our own little room with a view of the mountains in the distance. There're several comfortable looking chairs, a bench underneath the window, and a large bed in the middle of the room. Before we can do anything but set our bags down, our nurse comes in.

"Hey guys, I'm Annabel. I'll be with you for the next ten-ish hours. How're you doing?"

"Good, so far," I say.

"Ok, well as soon as you change into your gown and sit in bed I can start your IV. I'll give you a bag of regular fluids first before starting the bag that has the medicine that will start labor." She bustles around the room getting things ready as I change behind the curtain. Her blonde curls bounce each time she takes a step. I slip into the blue hospital gown and fold my clothes carefully. It helps to keep my mind off what I am about to go through.

I slide the curtain away and hand Alex my clothes.

"Perfect. Now just sit down and get comfortable. I'll start your medications as soon as this IV is in. Hopefully we will be able to meet these babies soon!" Annabel sits next to me and carefully places my IV into my left hand. My pale skin makes it easy for her to see the veins. "And that's it! I'll check on you soon." She waves and leaves the room.

I look over at Alex and he smiles. He pulls out a big bag of candy from his bag and holds it up.

"Candy? Is it alright for me to eat before delivering?"

"I figure we can play some cards or watch some TV and eat candy for a while. You're going to need your strength, so I'm sure eating is fine. Scoot over."

I slide over in bed and make room for him to sit next to me. I pick out a long sour straw covered in sugar from the candy bag and watch Alex flip through the channels. We can't find anything worth watching, so we just sit together and enjoy being just the two of us for the last time.

I arch my back as another contraction hits. I try not to yell, but I can't help it. This pressure is unlike anything I have ever felt.

"The medication given to start labor can be rough on your body sometimes, hun. I'm so sorry." My nurse checks my monitors. "I'm going to have to ask you to try to sit still for a minute while I put the fetal monitors back on."

I clench my teeth and sit as still as I can. In between each contraction there is a little down time where I can take a breath and try to relax. But as my contractions get stronger that time grows closer together in between them. Before one fetal monitor is even placed, another contraction hits.

I clench my eyes shut and get lost in the pain.

"Does she need those on right now?" Alex's voice floats over to me from near my feet.

"She hasn't been progressing as quickly as she should be. Especially with the bump up in medications from her doctor. It's best to have these on so that we know how well the babies are doing. If their heart rates go down or they seem stressed, we may have to perform a cesarean section."

"Alex?" I reach my hand out and he grabs onto it. "I can't have a C-section."

"If the babies need you to, you might have to." He holds my hand and squeezes a little. As a contraction hits, I squeeze back, and he whimpers a bit. The nurse works around us, and the contractions, and finally places both fetal monitors on my stomach. They are about the size of the palm of my hand and have long stretchy straps that wraps around me. The straps dig into my back and press uncomfortably on my contracting stomach, especially because I have two of them. One sits above each of the girls and displays their heartrate on monitors near my bed. They are incredibly irritating, but I try to stay still so that they can do their job. I want to make sure that the girls are doing fine inside.

"Why did the doctor give me more medication so soon?" I ask.

"He's the only doctor willing to do a vaginal delivery of twins and his shift is ending in a few hours. I think he wants to make sure the babies are born while he's here, or you will automatically be given a C-section." Alex moves my hair out of my face. His fingers are warm and leave little trails of warmth across my cold forehead. With each contraction, I get colder and shake just a little more.

The door to my room opens but no one enters immediately. "Uh, can I come in?"

I turn to look at the door and see Finn standing, his back facing us.

"I'm all covered, but the contraction..." before I can finish my thought another one hits. This time I feel like I'm going to vomit. I roll onto my right side and dry heave a few times over the side of the bed.

"Is she ok?" Finn's face loses all its color and he stays near the door.

"I'm fine, butthead. Get in here." I smile. Having him here makes me happy. Despite how I must look, and how terrible I feel, knowing that Finn is here calms me down just a little.

"When are you getting the epidural?" He creeps into the room and sits down next to the window.

"I hadn't thought of it for a while." I wonder why it hadn't popped into my head before now. I know I had wanted to try it all natural, but that was before I felt these contractions.

Another one hits, and I scream. It's stronger than ever before. I'm sure my body is being ripped apart. Tears stream down my face and I know that I need to do something to make this stop. I roll from my back and lay on my right side. The pain is different, but still just as strong. I try to sit up, but that doesn't feel any better either.

"Get the anesthesiologist, now!" Finn's voice booms into the hallway. I glance at him and his face is green.

Alex holds my hand and gives me a drink of water. "You're doing amazing. Finn has called for the anesthesiologist to come up here, but you can say no to the epidural if you really want."

"I want it now. Right now."

"They're on their way. Just try to breathe."

An hour goes by before the anesthesiologist gets to my room. I'm completely exhausted. The contractions have only gotten worse. I don't know how I'm going to have enough energy to deliver both babies. A cesarean seems like the only way to safely give birth to the babies at this point.

"All I need you to do in lean over and try to keep your head as close to your knees as possible." The doctor pulls on gloves and gets a tray ready. I can't see the needle, something that I'm grateful for. I have heard that they are really long and a bit thick in order to allow a small catheter to be placed in the space between the spinal canal.

"I'm going to administer the epidural as soon as your next contraction is over. You will feel pressure and it might sting for just a second. I'm going to give you a single dose first to see how you do. If you need more I will place a catheter in."

I bend down as best I can and try to stay still while another contraction hits. The doctor rubs something onto my back. As the contraction slows and fades, I feel like some sort of ant has bitten my back. It stings and makes me want to rub the area. I feel some pressure on my back and then I feel something cold trickle down my leg.

"Is it supposed to feel cold?" I whisper, afraid to move.

"It can feel cold. Where do you feel it?" He asks, still pressing on my back.

"In my legs."

"That's just fine. I'm all done with this now, so try to lay down and get comfortable before you get too numb."

Alex walks back into the room and helps me lay down. I wiggle my toes and watch them move without feeling much. It's almost like I had been sitting on them and they fell asleep. Thankfully the numbness goes form my stomach down to my feet. The contractions must still be happening, but I don't feel them anymore.

I take a drink from my ice water and close my eyes. Being able to rest is the best feeling and before I know it, I start to drift off.

"Feeling better, hun?" A new nurse comes into my room.

"Yes. Much better."

"Your contractions are nearly right on top of each other. Your doctor is in the operating room. He wants to deliver in there just in case you need a cesarean or the babies need extra help. The room is much larger."

"Alex can come in with me, right?"

"Of course. He will have to stand by your head because there will be a lot of people in there, but he's welcome to be there. He can even cut the cords if he wants."

"How many people will be there?"

"Well it will be your doctor and me, then a team from the NICU for each baby just in case they need oxygen or something from being 3 weeks early, and then there will also be the anesthesiologist in case you need more medication, and maybe another nurse. Probably fifteen people."

"That is a lot." My face turns pink and I hope it will be all be over soon. "Well, let's go meet our girls." I smile nervously and hold Alex's hand while they push my bed towards the operating room.

Rays of early morning light filter through the hospital blinds. I roll over in bed and check the clock. It is 8:04 and I have been a mother for almost two days now. I peek over my bed railing and watch as the girls sleep. They are so small that I put them in the same hospital bassinet and there is plenty of extra room.

One of the babies starts to fuss and I lift her up into my arms. She only weighs four and a half pounds but is solid and warm. I love the way she feels snuggled up next to me. As soon as we are comfortable, the other girl starts to fuss. I pick her up slowly and nestle her next to me as well. They're so small that I can't really tell them apart yet, so I just make a quiet *shush*-ing sound and we all fall back to sleep.

"Tara?" Alex calls me. I open my eyes a little and smile at him.

"Hi," I say quietly. I don't want to wake the babies.

"The nurse wants to check on the three of you and I think it's time to nurse again."

"Ok, let her in." I sit up and unclasp my gown. Nursing was a little weird at first but since I have to do it every two hours, I'm getting used to it. I position the girls so one is on each side and they latch on their own. The nurse comes in and gives me a big smile.

"Let me make sure they are getting some milk," she says, pulling out her stethoscope and listening to the girls as they swallow. "They're doing so well. How are you feeling, momma?"

"I feel really good. The shower was so nice." I was finally able to shower last night. Something about fresh clothes, clean hair and the smell of soap made me feel like an entirely new person.

"I bet. How do you feel about going home in an hour?"

I'm too surprised to say anything. I knew that we would be going home today, but I thought it would be later. I try to think of everything we might need. I know we have the car seats and clothes and diapers and wipes. I think about all the help the nurses have been and how in an hour it will just be Alex and me. We will have to remember every feeding every two hours and every diaper change. If anything goes wrong, we will have to know how to fix it. I think about trouble breathing and choking hazards and SIDS. I don't know what I would do if anything happened to one of the girls.

"I freaked you out a little, didn't I?" Our nurse smiles and pats my hand.

"Yeah, a little." I take a deep breath and look down at the girls. They're asleep while nursing and seem so peaceful.

"Everything will be fine. Just focus on nursing right now and the doctor will come in with the discharge papers when they're ready."

I nod and brush the tops of the girls' head. Their hair is deep brown and silky. It's so soft that it almost feels like fur.

"You want me to go get the car ready?" Alex asks as he joins me on the bed.

"You think we can do this? Take care of two little tiny people every second of every day?" I ask nervously as I watch their faces.

"Yes, I do. You are an amazing mom already and I know that we can do it together." Alex reaches out for my hand and rubs small circles on my palm.

"If you bring our bags down and then bring up the car seats we will be all ready to go pretty soon."

"Ok. Just relax and I will be back soon." He packs all of our bags and gives the three of us each a kiss before leaving.

The girls finish nursing and I burp them at the same time. As they are snuggled up on my chest I rub their backs and sing them a little song. They reach out for each other and link their arms together. We stay like that until we get the discharge paperwork. A few signatures is all it takes and then we are on our way to the car.

I carefully clip in each car seat to their bases and I decide to ride in the back between the girls. I crawl into my spot, in the middle, and check on each baby. The buckles are in the right spot and they each have their own little blanket despite the warm weather. Being four and a half pounds, they have a tough time staying warm. The nurses told us to make sure to keep them in an extra layer of clothing until they get a bit bigger.

While I stare at them, I realize that I would do anything for them. Despite the upcoming sleepless nights and exhausting days, I know that they are perhaps the best thing I have ever done. I sing to them the Kookaburra lullaby and soak in their sweet presence.

"You don't seem nervous at all." Alex turns around from the driver's seat and watches us.

"I've just been running from my past for so long. So afraid of somehow becoming my mother despite the lack of drug addiction. But I've decided that I'm done running and being afraid of something like that. I know exactly what not to do, or say, and how not to act. My mother was a fitting example of that."

"When did you come to this conclusion?"

"I guess it has been bouncing around my head since the girls were born. It's a huge blessing to know what not to do. Our girls are going to have such a great life. I'll make sure of it."

Epilogue: 12 Months Later

I take the spray bottle and spray the rest of our artificial tree with essential oils to make it smell like Christmas. The smell of cinnamon and fir trees float through the entire house. Three big boxes sit in the living room, waiting for me to unpack them and begin decorating our cabin. The reds and greens, that seem to be the only color for the season, spill out of them and pile onto the floor. Scarves, mittens, stockings, and every type of wrapping paper makes a mountain of Christmas that the twins are playfully digging through.

Aurora picks up a huge stocking and puts it on like a hat. It falls down her entire face and even slips a bit over her shoulders.

"Sissy?" Lillian's eyes are wide as she watches Aurora walking around without being able to see. Aurora bumps into the boxes and falls over giggling. Lillian immediately finds another stocking and pulls it over her light brown curls and down her face.

"Momma!" she screams as she runs around bumping into things.

"What are you doing crazy girl?" I laugh and pull the stocking up so that I can see her crystal blue eyes.

She mumbles something that I can't quite understands and pulls the stocking back down her face.

"You guys are little weirdos." Alex says carrying another box labeled 'Christmas' from storage.

"Wee-dough!" Aurora says, pulling on Alex's pants leg.

"Yes, you are a weirdo." He pushes her back into the pile of Christmas and laughs as she disappears under all the stuff.

"This is the box with all the ornaments in it. Do you want to get the tree done before we have to get the girls in bed?"

"Sure. I bought some plastic ones that they could try to do and then we will put the ones that are a bit breakable up higher, so they can't reach them." I rummage in the pile and find some little feet sticking out. I pull on them and Lillian screams and laughs.

"Girls? Do you want to do put things on the tree with us?" I point to the tree and smile.

"Tree!"

Their little legs move so fast, but they still aren't quite running as they go to the tree. They touch the branches carefully and pull their hands back quickly as they realize the tree is a bit prickly.

I sit on the floor next to them and pull the box of ornaments towards me. "Come here girlies. Look what's in here." I open the box and push it towards them.

Red, gold, and silver plastic ornaments are on top. The girls' eyes get wide and they tentatively reach out to hold them.

"Go ahead! Pick them up." I encourage.

Their little hands have a tough time holding them and they drop to the floor. As they bounce all over the house the girls laugh and chase them. Wrapping their chubby little figners around them is difficult, but as soon as they do they throw them back into the empty box.

"Aurora, can you say 'RED'?"

"Roo!"

"Good job, honey! What about you, Lillian? Can you say, 'RED'?"

"Rug."

"Good job! Now do you want to help me put the red ornaments onto the tree. Look." I take a red orb and slowly put it on one of the lowest branches. I take another one and slowly model how to put it on the tree. I look back at the girls and smile at them.

"Come on." I hand each of them a small red ornament and point to the tree.

"You'll probably need to do the hook thing yourself." Alex says, from above us where he is stringing the white lights.

"I figured I would just re-do it once they're asleep."

Aurora balances hers onto some branches and turns to me, obviously proud of herself. I give her a quick kiss and hand her another one. Lillian throws hers at the tree, and surprisingly it sticks. She laughs and reaches for more.

Before long we have made it to the bottom of the box and pull another small one to us. I open it to find the more delicate ornaments inside. One is frosted glass with a wedding picture of Alex and me. It was a gift to us for our first Christmas as a married couple. I show the girls.

"Momma! Dada!" they say and touch our faces.

I pull out a few ceramic snowmen, a Santa that Finn painted when he was little, and a few handmade ornaments made with macaroni noodles. I show each one to the girls but end up packing most of them away again. I don't want them to break after having saved them for so long. A discolored little package catches my eye and I pull it out.

I unwrap it to find the bumblebee ornament. The same yellow and black paint, the same little wings, and the tiny scratched in heart. Just holding it brings me back to Santa's Village.

"Momma!" Aurora reaches up to see the ornament.

"Do you want to see something special? Come here girls."

They crowd around me with excited expressions on their faces. I kneel down, keeping the ornament covered, and say, "Where did it go?"

The girls look around on the floor for a few seconds before slapping my hands.

"You found it! Ok, now sit down because this is delicate and can break."

They sit nearly on top of each other and hold their hands out. Their tiny hands wiggle with anticipation as I hand the ornament first to Aurora and then to Lillian.

"Be soft. This is something very special from when Momma was little." I trace my fingers around the bee and tell them about the wings, the eyes, and even how the stinger can hurt you.

"Ouch!" Lillian says.

"Yes, big ouch if a bee stings you."

I take the ornament back from them and get lost in the memories of the day I got it. I can remember how cold my hands were when Mom handed me the ornament. Even standing by the fire for so long hadn't helped. I thought I would drop the present when she gave it to me.

"Kind of got lost there for a minute, huh?" Alex rubs my back and hands me the wrapping and box to put the bumblebee away.

"Yeah. I think I'm going to put it up this year." I circle the tree looking for a good spot for it. I don't want it to be the first thing you see, but I do want it to be visible.

"Sounds good. What about up here by the top? The girls won't be able to reach it and we can see it from the living room a bit." Alex reaches for the ornament and places it carefully on the tree.

"That's the perfect spot."

The girls quickly lose interest in the tree and run around the boxes looking for new and exciting things. Their laughter fills the house and takes away the lingering feelings I have linked to the bumblebee ornament. Without even meaning to, the girls not only helped me heal from my past but helped me morph into the type of mother I always wanted.

"Momma! Got you!" Aurora yells and runs past me.

"Let's go!" Lillian pulls on my hand.

"Let's go to bed girlies!" I chase after them and tickle them every time I get close to them. After a few minutes Alex helps me take them into our room. We change their diapers, get their new Christmas pajamas on them, and lay them down.

After prayers and a story, I lay in between them and sing songs to them. Just before they fall asleep, they reach out for me and we hold hands until we all fall asleep in a pile together.

Acknowledgements

I am eternally grateful to my husband, Alex, who never gave up on me. From hearing these stories in late night phone calls when I was fifteen to encouraging me to write them down; there was nothing but support and love given to me. And when the endless revisions and drafts were frantically pressed into his hands, he took the time to read them, critique them, and encourage me.

To Gibbs: thank you for always being a rock amid the storm. You are my best friend, the worlds best uncle, and will always be my little brother.

A special thank you goes out to Joshua Hill for teaching creative writing to a group of unruly teenagers, who probably didn't show any appreciation at the time. It made all the difference in my life when the passion of telling stories, writing them down, and letting others see them had fallen to the side. Hearing your writing and sharing my own helped to spark that fire within me again.

For always lending a sympathetic ear and the promise of a pizza night at the end of a long quarter, thank you Jim Brown.

And lastly, to Paula Priamos: Without your endless dedication to a young student's story, this book would not have been possible. The time spent reading drafts, asking questions, encouraging me, and always pushing me forward despite your own many projects and busy teaching schedule truly impacted not only the book but my life. I have gained an amazing mentor and friend in you and can never thank you enough.

About the Author

Tara Cummins was born and raised in the mountains of Southern California. She received her MFA from California State University of San Bernardino and has taught at Victor Valley College. She now lives with her husband and four children in Salt Lake City, Utah. Her memoir, Mother's Ingredients, was published in 2020. Find her on Instagram at taralcummins or her website at taraleecummins.com.